The 30-Day Journey
to Loving
the Woman in Me

Reyna Joy Banks

ISBN 978-1-64492-212-5 (paperback)
ISBN 978-1-64492-213-2 (digital)

Christian Faith Publishing, Inc.
832 Park Avenue
Meadville, PA 16335
www.christianfaithpublishing.com

Printed in the United States of America

CONTENTS

PREFACE

This book, *The 30-Day Journey to Loving the Woman in Me*, was born in a season of my life where I felt myself falling apart and feeling so drained from being there for everyone else, constantly pouring out when there was no one around to pour back into me. I felt like I had lost everything because I could no longer love freely from all the hurt and pain that had come upon my life; not to mention, I lost the one thing that I only knew how to do with all my heart: the ability to love past my own understanding. There were many sleepless nights and tears. They were from a place so deep, only God could help bring me understanding. The pain came from a place of not knowing why it hurt so much to do what truly defined me as a woman, which was one of the only things I knew how to do naturally, in God's strength: the gift to *love*!

Because I was losing sight of my first love—Jesus—I began to love in my own strength. Yet in my own strength, I am not strong enough to love anyone or anything in the way I was called to…or even how I was used to. I was lacking in understanding regarding how to even *love myself* the way God had ordained and intended me to. This was apparent when I was throwing myself into audition after audition, gig after gig, ministry after ministry, and keeping myself so busy that I couldn't even take a moment to feel the *love* that had been lost and tucked away so deeply inside of me.

Being a dancer, actress, voiceover talent, host (radio and TV), choreographer, creative director, visionary, producer, inspirational speaker, and CEO in the entertainment industry, I deal with rejection on a daily basis. I face pressure, anxiety, stress, feelings of inadequacy, and sometimes, even come to a place to where I feel like I'm never going to be enough even though God has equipped me for it and says: "You are *more than enough* and capable of doing all I have called you to do and be!" This includes my family, relationships, and

5

destiny. I am being pulled on all the time and need to make things happen—and fast—in the most excellent way. So my joy was gone, and I no longer knew how to enjoy alone time with God, never mind do something fun for myself, which is a huge part of loving myself, stress free.

In the midst of all of this, there came a point when I finally looked up and realized I had lost sight of what was most important. It wasn't about the size of the next check; it was about the number of souls that experienced the presence and love of God any time he had me step foot on a set, a stage, or even into a production meeting to create another one of his masterpieces. I needed a wake-up call, and I needed it once and for all to begin the journey to loving myself the way God had always intended. Only then could I help so many others be set free into their destinies!

See, God's love is without motives, expectations, assumptions, boasting, blemish, and limitations. God's love is unconditional, ever-lasting, indefinable, limitless, sound, forgiving, real, and above all, it's everything. Just as God had me ask myself this question, I will now do the same and ask you: What is keeping you from falling in *love* with yourself?

You may not be able to answer this question just yet, but I challenge you to write it down in your journal (go to the Pre-Journal section in your 30-Day Journal), and when it comes to the appointed time…, you will be able to answer this question and allow God to *restore* all that was lost. Then *you can begin to love again* and you can *love* yourself *just the way you are!*

The 30-Day Journey to Loving the Woman in Me is a day-by-day process to help you take the steps necessary to be released into loving yourself in the way that is needed in order to be free, healed, and able to love others all around you, beyond your own understanding. Most of you might be thinking: *I do love myself; I love me some me; I am all for me; and I take care of myself!* But my question to you is: How do you know you truly, genuinely, and whole-heartedly love yourself? Before you answer that question, take a look back at your past seasons in life and even some of your current seasons in your life.

The life of love, most say, isn't supposed to hurt; it's supposed to give life and breath—a sense of strength into everyone around us. But at the same time, when someone is loving in the midst of hurting and never healing…, the will to love becomes a strain, and then the joy of it is fully taken away. This is the complete opposite of what defines the love that we know we are supposed to endure and spread around the world, give to the people around us, and most of all, pour into ourselves.

The truth is, when we are wounded and have not healed from our past, we can love, but we love with expectations, which will always lead to being let down in some way, by someone. Or as soon as something happens that reminds us of the past, we shut down or ball our fist up to fight; when in actuality, there is no one to fight but the inner part of our being that keeps us held to the things of the past that we need to release and be free from.

Even if someone came around to love you, you would most likely not be open to receive it because the feeling of loving yourself has to start with you and understanding God's love for you. You have to understand the effect that love has on us, even when we force it or deny it. It's as if we have lost a piece of ourselves for however long that season may be because love is a part of our make-up and defines the truth in how this world and our lives are supposed to be. We function off the life of love, and the truth is that a life without love is lost and close to being dead and empty.

So when you look in the mirror, what do you see? Can you openly say: "I love me some me?" What is holding you back from taking the time you need to understand yourself, get to know your-self, be alone with yourself, and most importantly, *love yourself*? How will you choose to live? How will you choose to bring forth a shift to set in position your full "30-day Journey to Loving Me"?

Being able to love yourself begins with forgiving yourself for anything that you feel you allowed to hurt you. It wasn't your fault. Say this out loud: "It wasn't my fault," and "I want to be free." In saying this, it begins now. Your healing to love again starts now, and it starts with *The 30-Day Journey to Loving the Woman in Me*.

Step-by-step and day-by-day, I, with God's guidance, will help you get to that place by taking you on a journey of understanding the truth of what it takes to truly and wholeheartedly *loving yourself.* You may not want to go to certain places emotionally, but if you really want a change to come, you have to go to some of the most uncomfortable, darkest places and moments that tainted your love for yourself and the love that God is offering to you. You must allow God to shine his light on each wound and scar so you can be wiped clean and set free to love and be loved for eternity.

Things you will need during this journey:

1. *The 30-Day to Journey Loving the Woman in Me* Journal
2. A special pencil or pen
3. A box of tissue (a huge one)
4. Your Bible (If you don't have one, email me: The30DayJourneyToLovingMe@gmail.com)
5. Pandora—you can listen at www.pandora.com (I recommend the William McDowell station)
6. iTunes Radio (I recommend the Relaxation and Meditation Station)
7. Share your Journey with other women all over the world by reading below:

Join Me on Social Media

As you begin to take on this journey and journal, your *process into your breakthrough*, you should be aware that you are not alone during this process. It was placed on my heart to allow social media to be a tool for us to help other women all over the world become free through our healing.

When I posted my *#TransparencyMoment* periodically throughout the week and months in obedience to God, I realized how many women were relating to me and beginning to become free through my *process into my breakthrough*.

The comments, messages, tears, truths, wounds, and healings that came forth made me want to keep going, even when I was ready to give up. It was in those moments that I knew this wasn't just about me, but also about every woman across this nation and world becoming whole, healed, and free to step into their destiny.

In your journal, every day has a "hashtag" associated with it so feel free to use that hashtag when you share your journey on social media. You can tag me in your posts, and we can participate together. So as you begin *journaling your journey,* I challenge you to join me in *"hashtagging"* your *days (as you will see in your journal),* your *transparency moments,* and *posting* about your powerful moments as you live out *The 30-Day Journey To Loving The Woman In You.*

Join me:
Instagram: @ReynaJoy
Twitter: @ReynaJoyBanks
Facebook: Reyna Joy Banks
Let's go there so you will never be the same!
Say: "It's time for *me* to be *free* and *loving* the *woman* in *me!*"

I challenge you to take your own special thirty days to getting familiar with yourself and transitioning from being so much about everyone else to instead putting yourself first. This will be just for a little while to see how you can affect, infect, and birth the new and whole you who is strong, passionate, solid, whole, and *loved* by God and yourself. You'll be able to receive love from others in a genuine, pure-hearted way.

PART 1

The Process

*Then said Jesus unto them, "When ye have lift up the Son of man,
then shall ye know that I am he, and that I do nothing of myself;
but as my Father hath taught me, I speak these things.
And he that sent me is with me: the Father hath not left me alone;
for I do always those things that please him." As he
spake these words, many believed in him.*

—John 8:28–30, KJV

DAY 1

Rest

My soul finds rest in God alone. My salvation comes
from Him. He alone is my rock and my salvation;
He is my fortress; I will never be shaken.

—Psalm 62:1–2 (NKJV)

You may be wondering why chapter 1 of *The 30-Day Journey to Loving the Woman in Me* is starting out with *rest*. Most of the time, when you are running yourself thin and going, going, going without thought of what you need and only thinking about what others need from you, you do not or are not getting rest! From not resting comes stress, from stress comes exhaustion, and from exhaustion comes a whole new cycle of people-pleasing and never *restoring* from all that you have poured out and allowing it to be poured back into you. This is what *rest* does for us when we allow it to. And in the midst of our *rest*, God does his greatest work.

My *30-Day Journey to Loving the Woman in Me* started with exactly this: *rest* because in actuality, it was all I had left to give. It was all I physically, mentally, emotionally, and spiritually had the energy left to do. I had found myself in a place of not only exhaustion but felt like I wanted to give up completely. Yes! Give up! Give up on my destiny, family, relationships, and my God-ordained career—or I should say *calling*. I found myself in a place of getting on my knees and not being able to pray, let alone worship my Heavenly father who gave his only son for me. My joy was nowhere to be found, and my peace wasn't surpassing a thing because it no longer had grounds in my daily life. This was a sign to me that something had to change—and not for a season—but for eternity.

> Humble yourselves, therefore, under the mighty
> hand of God so that at the proper time he may
> exalt you, casting all your anxieties on him,
> because he cares for you. (1 Peter 5:6–7, KJV)

My tears became a part of my daily living. There wasn't a night that I went to sleep without crying. I also didn't have a dry eye throughout the day. I felt like I was dying, but—remember this and pay attention—I felt like I was dying physically, having no idea at the time that I was actually dying to self for God to rule and reign in victory over my life eternally.

At that point, I knew I needed to talk to someone; someone I could trust with any and everything I had to say, so that I could truly begin to release from the depths of all that was beginning to make me fade away. Harmony Samuels, my big brother in Christ, made time for me (in the midst of his busy schedule) to meet with him immediately and allowed the Holy Spirit to guide our time. It was as if God had prepared him for me and allowed my brother to hear my heart's cry. The moment I walked into his amazing recording studio, I felt the peace of God for the first time in a long time. I knew that marked the day and moment in time when I was going to begin to allow myself to be free.

Stop here and turn to Journal No. 1 in your journal and follow the exercises before moving on to the next paragraph.

My *rest* was the first thing that God used to begin my process of *the 30-Day Journey to Loving the Woman in Me.* He sat me down and showed me *"the me"* I was always intended to be and then showed me *"the me"* I was living as so carelessly. I know that many of you can relate to this when I confessed I was saying "yes" to pretty much everything and everybody…and it got to the point where my life became other people's agenda versus God's agenda. In my own strength, I was trying to make everything work, even when some things were just not meant to work because God never intended for them to be a part of my life…or the story he wrote for me.

You see, most people say, "I'll sleep when I die." But to *rest* is to *restore*, and without *rest*, your *restoration* can't take place, and if *restoration* doesn't take place, then you are using what's left of yesterday's energy to complete a new day. It just simply won't work. *You will burn out!*

So when I heard the Lord say, "Rest, Reyna, rest!" I *rested* in him and him alone. Realizing why I wasn't resting and then saying, "Enough is enough," was when I finally surrendered, submitted, and said *yes* to God's *rest*. What got me the most is how I felt when I woke up; it was one step closer to being free because my eyes were dry, and the burdens I was carrying became light.

The revelation in *resting* became so much clearer and more consistent. In that I became less stressed, less overwhelmed, more creative, full of peace that surpasses all understanding (Philippians 4:7), and filled with true joy that only comes from the Lord. I said to myself, "It can only get easier from here." At least, that is what I had thought. As soon as you make a verbal declaration and bring your mind and body into submission to your spirit, to *rest* and begin to be *restored* by God and only through God, it's as if a tug-of-war begins between the flesh and the spirit.

It's like you are needed by multiple people at the same time, every hour on the hour. You begin to worry and think about all the bills you have, or all the work that you need to get done before Friday comes. Three Ss: *Stop, Sit,* and make your mind *Submit.* Turn off your cell phone, place your home phone on silent, and begin to write in your journal as a form of worship.

Stop and Journal

#DAY1
#REST

"My soul finds REST in God alone.
My salvation comes from Him.
He alone is my rock and my salvation;
He is my fortress; I will never be shaken"
(Psalms 62:1-2 NKJ)

JOURNAL #1:

1. Who is it that keeps you from being set free?

2. What is it that keeps you from being set free?

3. When will you allow yourself to be set free?

Stop, sit, and make your mind submit!

JOURNAL #2:

1. What keeps you from resting?

2. What keeps you from loving yourself enough to say, "I need my rest?"

3. What keeps you from truly loving yourself just as much as you love others?

Before I go deeper into answering these questions, I need you to understand that this book is not to tell you what you have to do, nor is it to give you the answers to your problems. I am not God in any way, shape, or form. But what I will tell you is that he wants you to understand that it is okay to start loving yourself. This is just the blueprint for how to really start to do that in the most effective, breathtaking, and life-changing ways. He wants you to understand *the you* that he is so in love with, and he wants you to take the time to embrace that he is calling you to do some amazing things. But it all starts with the time you take in getting to know yourself, understanding yourself, and most importantly, beginning to love yourself the way God does and intended you to do. So here we go.

1.   What keeps you from *resting*?

Speaking from the experience in the awakening that happened inside of me when I realized I didn't like to *rest* or even desire to *rest* or wouldn't allow myself to *rest*, I was fighting the people-pleasing syndrome of being unavailable when people needed me the most. I was overextending myself to the point of triple booking my schedule, just so I didn't have to say *no*!

Saying *no* is one of the hardest things for a person, especially for a woman to do in the midst of trying to be more than enough to and for everybody throughout each season of our lives. But saying *no* is one of the greatest gifts that God could've ever given us because it keeps us from walking out of alignment with where we are supposed to be and doing what we are supposed to be doing for him and ourselves in that very moment.

So what keeps you from *resting*? The ability to say *no* without an explanation. In being able to say *no* to people, we are, in return, saying *yes* to God and his will for us in that moment of that hour on that day. Hold onto this; we will come back to "The People-Pleasing Syndrome" and "The Power in Saying No!"

2.   What keeps you from *loving yourself* enough to say, "I need my *rest*"?

The first question I have to ask myself is: what does loving myself have to do with me *resting*? It has everything to do with it. Being willing to *rest* is saying: I realize I have poured out a lot of myself today, and the only way I can continue to do that is to allow myself to be *restored* from all I gave to so many people around me.

Let's go a little deeper. Loving yourself is saying and admitting that you have done a lot, and part of that is listening to what your body is telling you concerning the wear and tear of all that you have done. In order to listen to the voice of your body, you must submit your mind to that voice and submit them both to your spirit. The Holy Spirit is always speaking; the question is: are you open to hear what he has to say to you? And are you willing to be *obedient*? The first step to loving yourself is understanding God's love for you, and then from there, you can begin to submit to the heart of real *rest*.

3. What keeps you from truly *loving yourself*, just as much as you love others?

I had to ask myself: why don't I feel like I matter to myself as much as others matter to me? Why don't I feel like I am as important to myself as others are important to me? But the greatest question is: why can't I love myself as much as I choose to unconditionally love others? There it is. Now, reread those questions really quick before moving on.

Making yourself a priority is not defined as being selfish; in actuality, it's being selfless because you're saying *I want to be the best me for God, myself, and all those around me, so I must take the time necessary to be restored and rested in order for God to do a greater work inside and through me.* Basically, God is saying, "I need time with you in order for you to be any good for anyone else! Allow me to pour my love into you so it can flow through you to all those around you!" It's never by our own might or our own strength, and once we get that, we will understand the fullness of what *rest* was intended for in the first place. You matter, and until you realize that, you will only be able to reach a quarter of the capacity of all that God has called you to be and do.

Open yourself up to receive what is coming in this 30-Day Journey to Loving the Woman in You. It's *resting* your *mind, heart, body,* and *spirit* so you can receive the fullness of the love that God is drawing you into, in order for you to be *restored*. Resting in God is the first true step to the thirty-day journey to loving the woman in *you*!

DAY 2

Defining Moments

A memorable, life-changing decision, event, or
action that alters the course of our life.

—Greg Nemer

Day 2 is not as simple as *rest* seemed to be. Today, *rest* does not appear to exist as much, and you find yourself in serious *defining moments*. For me, I slipped back into old habits of overextending myself beyond my human abilities; I became a "Yes Wo-Man" and forgot about what? "Loving the woman in me!" This is the day that you truly *stop* and say, "If I want to fully begin to *love myself*, I must make myself unavailable to many things and focus in on 'Me' things."

As mentioned on day one, there comes a point where "No" has to become your best friend because it protects you from exhaustion and emptiness. This is your time to be *filled, rejuvenated,* and *restored,* not pulled in fifty different directions and then left speechless at the end of the day when you ask yourself: "What did I do for *myself* today?" Or what I ask myself: "Lord, what did I do for *us* today?"

I can almost *promise* you that most people are not going to like your decision on this, nor will they agree with it, but what matters most on this day is beginning to set the tone for all the days to come. You do this by grabbing a hold of your strength through God so that you can handle each individual in the best way possible and start to matter to yourself and others the way you matter to God. This is when "People-Pleasing" has to be put to shame once and for all.

19

You may say, "I'm not a people-pleaser," but most likely, if you are reading this book and can relate in any way, there is a fifty percent chance that you battle with this major people-pleasing syndrome. The people-pleasing must be stopped in order for you to fully begin to please God. This will allow others (from the outside, looking in) to begin to understand what it means to truly experience *defining moments* through your desire to please God versus them.

Stop and Journal

#DAY2
#DEFININGMOMENTS

"A memorable, life changing decision, event, or
action that alters the course of our life."
—Greg Nemer

JOURNAL #3:

1. Write down what your definition of the "People-pleasing Syndrome" is:

"But without faith it is impossible to please him: for he that cometh to God must believe that he is, and that he is a rewarder of them that diligently seek him."

(Hebrews 11:6 KJV)

I never saw myself as the type of person who cared about what people thought, but I was that person who cared about everyone else—so much—so that I didn't have a voice anymore, know what made me smile, or did the little things that made me enjoy living life. What I have always enjoyed the most in my life is hearing the voice of the Lord, spending intimate time with him, and being available to be used by him in any way shape or form at *any time*. But even *that* was little to non-existent at that point in my life.

This was a *defining moment* for me in so many ways. No matter what, you have to set boundaries with everyone, and in every area of your life—including family—in order to be the best you for God, them, and yourself. If you give all of yourself away, then you have nothing left to give to yourself…you have nothing left to give to your Heavenly father. Begin to understand what the scripture says about seeking him: "But seek ye first the kingdom of God and his righteousness; and all these things shall be added unto you" (Matthew 6:33, KJV).

Why seek him? Because when we begin to understand that seeking God is just as important as reporting to our boss on a job, we will feel less bound and more free to do all we are called to; we are only doing what God has given us the greatest ability to do. That's what it means when we say to love in God's strength and not in our own because we aren't strong enough without him to truly love anyone the way he intended for us in the capacity he has called us to. *You* are included in that type of love: *for you to love yourself.*

Let's go back to the "People-Pleasing Syndrome" and how it was defined in my life. People-Pleasing is not being able to say *no* so everyone else is happy; it's doing something just so no one gets upset or let down. An example: answering your phone every time someone calls, even though you're so exhausted. Caring about other people is important. As a matter of fact, that's the only way most of us know how to live. But it is *a must* that you care with God's love and in his strength as he guides you to do so—not in your own strength—and overextending yourself past what he gives you permission to do.

What God had me do was reevaluate what I was doing for others, for myself, and for him. He wanted me to step outside of myself and look at the reasons why I was so exhausted and stressed to the point of not being able to *rest* or *create* because my mind was never at ease. Does this sound familiar to you at all? This is not a knock at you or even your character, but it is a wake-up call for you, just as God did for me. It's for you to have a second, third, or however many chances you need to take time to understand, know, accept, and grow to love yourself.

Stress is another key setback on day two that can try to destroy you with one to too many yeses, and in this season of your life, those yeses can end up costing you your life. You *must* matter. Why? Because *you* matter! You are important to God and so many people whether you know it or not. Now, it's time you become important to yourself as well. In order for others to treat you with a little importance and show that you matter, you must see yourself in the same light as God sees you. People can only do what we allow them to do.

During this time, I had to ask myself, "When are you going to stop allowing people to not understand your worth and begin to appreciate yourself for all that God has called you to be and do here on this earth for him and for others?" This was another *defining moment* for me; I realized I wanted to be needed by someone or something and try to fix people's problems in order to be okay or to feel affirmed, valuable, and even important to myself. How did I realize this? It was because any time I was alone, my joy and peace were altered. Any time I wasn't being pulled in fifty directions, I forced myself into new projects and became flustered when I should have been resting. When God would tell me to sit down, I couldn't, and when he told me to do something, I wouldn't because I was already all over the place, trying to save the world just to feel affirmed, valuable, and important! Wow!

How many of you just felt your heart drop and possibly a tear fall? I'm crying even now because I had to realize first, that I felt I wasn't enough, in order for God to then come in and show me, day-by-day, night-by-night, and tear after tear that I was more than enough. I was more than enough in just being the *me* he had created me to be. But I had to begin to love myself in order to begin to see that *true me.*

> But without faith it is impossible to please him:
> for he that cometh to God must believe that he
> is, and that he is a rewarder of them that dili-
> gently seek him. (Hebrews 11:6, KJV)

I began to *seek* him before saying "Yes" and even before saying "No." I stayed on my knees a little bit longer and read the Word a little bit deeper. I fought to put my cellphone away, and sometimes laid on my face, crying out to no longer live for people or even for myself but to grab ahold of all God was calling me to be.

Sometimes, we have to go to that place we never wanted to go and be vulnerable with God and say, "Forgive me for trying to be you for others and not allowing you to use me continuously from stepping in your way. Forgive me for being so focused on pleasing others instead of pleasing you, Lord, and not allowing myself to be available to you for you to do a greater work through me for your glory."

> The Righteous cried out, and the Lord hears them; He delivers them from all their troubles. (Psalms 34:17, NIV)

In return, God spoke to me many times, saying,

> I am yours, and you are mine. I chose you before you were able to choose me, and I know your heart, my daughter. I know your weakness and your strengths. I know every tear you've cried, and every life you've tried to save as your cup ran dry. But if you allow me to, I will show you what it means to have my peace that surpasses all understanding, and my joy that is never-ending. I will use you for my glory, but I need you to trust me and begin to draw nearer to me so you can love Me the way I limitlessly love you. I will restore you. Come to me and I will give you rest, and I will make your name great for My glory as you worship Me through your love for My people."

This was everything, and in this very *defining moment*, I knew this 30-day journey was just the beginning of understanding my true destiny and how God desired to use me for his kingdom. So now, I want you to ask yourself: "What is God desiring of *me* in this season?"

Stop and Journal

JOURNAL #4:

1. What can I do to die to the "People-pleasing Syndrome" and instead live to please God?

2. What boundaries do I need to set concerning certain people, and even ministries?

3. What am I doing now that's for God? For myself? For others?

4. What have been some "Defining Moments" for me while reading Day Two?

5. How can I start the change to begin the journey to loving me?

"The righteous cry out, and the Lord hears them;
he delivers them from all their troubles."

(Psalm 34:17 NIV)

DAY 3

The Truth

Then you will know the truth, and the truth shall set you free.

—John 8:32 (NIV)

Day 3 is when the *truth* about you becomes clearer. Just as I started to, you will begin to learn things about yourself that you didn't even know help you, strengthen you, push you, defined you, and make you *you*. You wake up to a joy that has no reason or even makes sense, but it's what you're so full of. You find the moments of power where you feel so free to giggle and speak to random people who you may never see again. You begin sharing your joy with those who pass you by, leaving a positive effect on all those who can see your light truly shine.

There's work to be done, but the moment that it becomes too much and your joy is shifted, you find that place of peace, described on day two, and begin to do what? Place your cell on vibrate or silent, and just like on day one, *rest* until you wake naturally without tense direction and with joy outweighing everything else.

My mentor and sister, Faune Chambers-Watkins, once told me something, and I will never forget it: "It's not the *truth* that will set you *free*, but it's what you *do* with the *truth* that fully sets you *free!*"

This is in all areas of our lives; we must be willing to make a change and a move in the midst of what is revealed so we can truly walk into a better, healthier, and restful place. It isn't meant for you to hold onto things that never belonged to you in the first place. This could include: the person who told you that you would never amount to anything; the situation that almost cost you your life or your child's life; the man who never knew your worth; that pastor who didn't understand what he was speaking over you (and was never intended for you to live out); the doctor who said you had two months left to live; or the cancer that took control over your organs...God says, "Enough is enough." It's time to speak *truth* into your life. It's time to reverse every lie or circumstance that tried to latch itself onto you.

Every spirit and every demonic attack we bind right now in the name of *Jesus Christ*. Why? Because God calls you something else. He says something greater about you. He has chosen something so huge for you, and he is greater than all of those things, whatever they are. Therefore, don't give them life or even room to breathe in your body. Instead, say, "You have to go, and you don't belong here anymore! I am strong, I am beautiful, I am healed, and I am worth something more than what you say and have said about me. I am called, chosen, and destined for this because God said so. You must go now! In Jesus's name, amen!"

Stop and Journal

#DAY3
#THETRUTH

"Then you will know the truth, and the truth shall set you free."
(John 8:32 NIV)

JOURNAL #5:

1. What is it that you need to be truthful about while beginning this journey?

2. What keeps you from loving yourself?

3.   What keeps you to yourself, or keeps you afraid to be alone?

> "You are the light of the world. A city on a hill
> cannot be hidden. Neither do people light a lamp
> and put it under a bowl. Instead they put it on its
> stand, and it gives light to everyone in the house.
> In the same way, let your light shine before men,
> that they may see your good deeds and praise
> your Father in heaven."
>
> (Matthew 5:14-16 NIV)

This is when you really begin to start journaling and only journaling the *truth;* it's between you and God alone. I am saying this
because when I began to journal again, I realized it was a huge part of
my healing process and finally understood why I had stopped journaling for years. I didn't want to face the *truth* about what was still
hurting me and hindering my capability of fully *loving* myself. So
take the time you need to journal every wound, every hurt, every
cry, every heartache, and every person who impacted your life in a
way that has kept you from truly living to your full potential, from
forgiving, and from *loving* yourself. It's time to tell the *truth* so you
can *heal.*

I had to do the same thing, and I am so happy I did. You will
soon read my story, but first, I want you to write pieces of yours
down so that as I go through mine, you can begin to let the layers of
your wounds unfold and fall off for good.

You are somebody, and you mean so much to God. You must
understand that and begin to live in it. No matter how hard you have
to fight to be free, or how many nights you cry in order to begin to
heal, it's all worth it because there is a *you* on the inside that the world
is waiting to see so they can begin to believe that there is a God who
loves them so deeply. It's time for you to allow the light of *the you*
God always intended you to be to shine all the way through. You are
destined, and there is only one *you.* Don't leave this place without a

legacy in your name for God's glory. The next chapters may not get easier, but I promise that you will soon be free to shine.

> You are the light of the world. A city on a hill cannot be hidden. Neither do people light a lamp and put it under a bowl. Instead they put it on its stand, and it gives light to everyone in the house. In the same way, let your light shine before men, that they may see your good deeds and praise your Father in heaven. (Matthew 5:14–16, NIV)

DAY 4

Is It Real?

*Real: Not imitation or artificial; genuine
Synonyms: actual, nonfictional, factual, real-
life (from Google's definition of "real")*

Day 4 is when you understand the reality of what happened in day three and take it all in so that it doesn't just become another "Truth Moment" but becomes your reality. It's another *defining moment* on this journey and a true glimpse of your *ultimate destiny.*

Yesterday may have brought forth some really painful memories and some unforgivable moments in your life that shaped you in a way where it has been impossible for you to love yourself—or to even allow anyone else to love you. Believe me when I say it is okay. But what I can't allow you to do anymore is hold onto the things that keep you from forgiving. We don't forgive for the person; we forgive for ourselves because when un-forgiveness is in our heart, it limits the move of God in our lives. It's hindering him from being able to do what he desires to do for you, with you, and through you. Yes, he is God, and he can do "exceedingly abundantly above all that we ask or think, according to the power that worketh in us" (Ephesians 3:20, KJV). But what he won't do is allow you to feel comfortable in holding a grudge or holding onto something that was meant to keep you stagnant or captive. Not forgiving shows him that you aren't quite ready for the best that he has for you.

Let's look at it like this: every time we fail and ask for forgiveness with or without true repentance (we'll go deeper into this later on),

God, without question or hesitation, still forgives us for every sin. He sent his son so we could be blameless before him, our Heavenly father. So who am I and who are we to not forgive someone else! No matter how great or small the situation, we must forgive and release it into the hands of our Lord.

> Let all bitterness, and wrath, and anger, and clamour, and evil speaking, be put away from you, with all malice: And be ye kind one to another, tenderhearted, forgiving one another, even as God for Christ's sake hath forgiven you. (Ephesians 4:31–32, KJV)

For some reason, the Lord had me touch on that because it's a very important process of this journey, and without it, more than half of this book would be in vain. Transformation won't happen without the understanding and action of forgiving with a pure heart. Freedom is in forgiveness, and forgiveness is a huge part of freedom. Do you want to be free? Then I challenge you, one day at a time, to learn how to forgive others as God has—and he still continually forgives you.

Enjoy this process, enjoy your journey, and enjoy the ins and outs of *you,* along with all that has brought you to this place of who you are today. A new place within yourself, where you can pick up a book like this and finally know that it is okay to be you…, and that it's possible to finally begin the journey to *loving yourself.*

Stop and Journal

#DAY4
#ISITREAL

Real: 2. not imitation or artificial; genuine
Synonyms: 1. actual, nonfictional, factual, real-life
(Google definition of "real")

JOURNAL #6:

1. What was the hardest part for you yesterday?

2. When did you feel the strongest?

3. What made you most uncomfortable?

4. What kept you wanting to press forward on your journey?

5. Can you see yourself loving you?

> "I can do all things through Christ which strengtheneth me." (Philippians 4:13 KJV)

> And he who sits on the throne said,
> "Behold, I am making all things new." And he said,
> "Write, for these words are faithful and true."
> (Revelation 21:5, NIV)

Even in the midst of meditating on yesterday and reflecting on the beginning of your breakthrough, you must realize how vulnerable you could be and how open you are to be attacked in some way, shape, or form. Why? Because you did exactly what the enemy didn't want you to do. You went back to that place of hurt to begin your restoration and ultimately, to be fully healed. Yesterday is as real as it gets, but yesterday was yesterday and today is today... So my question to you, as it was for me, is: "What's real for you today?"

For me, on day four, I felt a true sense of peace and joy that I hadn't felt in a long time—or possibly ever. I woke up feeling a sense of freedom and asking myself: "Is this real?" I asked this because I had been living in brokenness for so long, I couldn't remember what it felt like to smile genuinely and be stress free in an unforced way. I had become so numb to being exhausted, overworked, under pressure, complacent, and especially discouraged.

My uncle, Chuck Singleton, told a life-changing story in service at Loveland Church one day. He said, "Satan and his demons were having a yard sale one day, and Satan told them to get rid of everything except for one of his greatest tools that works every time on God's children without getting them to openly sin. A tool that steals their joy, hope, and peace, and questions their faith. That tool is *discouragement*. And Satan said, 'If I can't get them with anything else, this one tool always works.'"

That story was all I needed to remember when it comes to fighting off numbness. It reminded me to latch onto what my Heavenly father says about you and me: "I can do all things through Christ which strengthens me" (Philippians 4:13, KJV).

At that very moment, God had given me a profound encounter with himself—just as he is doing for you, right now, in this very moment. You are no longer subject to what you used to be and how you used to feel. You are submitting to the call for your journey to wholeness and being free from all iniquities. I know this because you are still reading, and it's what God says concerning you. You act as if you are so you will be. You act as if you are free so you become free in Christ Jesus. There is so much more to you than the eyes can see, and I must tell you this, if you are asking yourself the same question I did: "Is this real?"

God's answer to you is, "Yes, it is real!" It is very real, and you are right where you're supposed to be, in this very moment, feeling the exact way you should.

Now, there may be some of you who aren't quite feeling what I felt when I woke up on this day. The tears may have doubled; the anger may have resonated from remembering those defining moments from the past, and the pain may have deepened. If this is where you're at, it's okay. It truly is okay because you are human, and some things just aren't that simple to release and be free from—at least—in your own strength. In God's strength, all things are easier done than even spoken. You were chosen to go through your circumstance and come out of it. I know this because God will never allow us to be tempted beyond what we can handle or bear (*1 Corinthians 10:13, KJV*). Just as with Job, everything has a purpose for God to reveal himself to you in the most humbling and breathtaking way. I'm speaking only from example.

Before I decided enough was enough, and before God took me on this thirty-day journey to loving me, I went back and forth with those feelings, not able to let God come in and heal me. So what I did was fix myself on certain scriptures. I promise you, if you can do the same and are open to this, and really want to be free, it will get you to that place of having full joy and peace, authentically and limitlessly.

Stop and Journal

JOURNAL #7:

Please read:

- Romans 12:2
- Jeremiah 29:11
- 1 John 4:4
- Lamentations 3:23
- Isaiah 40:31

How are you feeling now? Be honest:

Your full joy and peace may not happen immediately. Possibly not even today or tomorrow, but what I do know is that it will happen as long as you say, *yes* to the "Process to Progress" and *no* to the "Pains of the Past." Remember: it's a new day, and every day that you read this book, you're becoming a new you. It's *a you* who's ready and willing to love you…And it's just the beginning!

What Will You Choose Your Reality to Be?

Your reality is whatever you want it to be, but I'm praying and hoping that you choose the path of *peace* and *joy* with God. With God, and through God, you will come to the place that overrides everything and becomes the true definition of everlasting. You *can* do this, and you *will* do it because God has already paved the way for you to overcome. It's just the three Ss again—the ones I touched on before.

Stop and Journal

JOURNAL #8: (Write down your own definitions for each word below.)

1. Stop:

2. Surrender:

3. Submit:

From the definition of "submit," that other person is *God!* When I said that he has you, I mean just that. He has you beyond what the eyes can see and words can define. Stand in this moment with the understanding that it is okay to be vulnerable and rest in his arms like never before.

DAY 5

True Breakthrough

Let your eyes look straight ahead, fix your gaze directly before you.
Make level paths for your feet and take only ways that are firm.

—Proverbs 4:25–26 (NIV)

On day 5, there are *steps* to your *True Breakthrough,* and those steps must be taken in order to get past this day of *grace.* In biblical context, the number five means *grace* (www.biblestudy.org), and God wants you to know that his grace has sustained you in the midst of it all. No matter where you've been, or what you've done, believe him. Paul explains this in God's Word: "But He said to me, 'My grace is sufficient for you, for my power is made perfect in weakness.' Therefore I will boast all the more gladly about my weaknesses, so that Christ's power may [REST] on me" (2 Corinthians 12:9, NIV).

Step 1: *Transparency* in the Midst of *Exhaustion*

Getting down to the nitty-gritty with yourself is crucial during this process, just as in days three and four; it's being *truthful* and *real* in order to step into the birthing of your *true breakthrough.* You need to have one or two great friends, who you are in covenant with spiritually and equally yoked, to stand with you and by you on this day because this is the day that *true truth* unfolds. A punch in the wall with cries of pain are just the bare minimum of what comes forth from the realization of what has been holding you hostage. Take a second and breathe. I'm asking you to do this because I can only get you to go as deep as you need to, in order to begin to be *free*, by telling you a piece of my story.

Before I do so, let's pray: *Dear heavenly Father, I humbly come before you, saying thank you for your love, mercy, grace, peace, joy, hope, strength, protection, and my faith in you that sustains me in the midst of it all. You are so worthy, Lord, of all the glory and praise. And Lord, I'm saying right now that I need you more than ever. Father, I need you to meet us in this moment to break down that wall so we can release the depths of our cries and pain. I want to be free; they want to be free; we want to be free! Lord, speak your love to us through this moment and allow us to see your heart and understand the truth in it all so we can understand that it was all for such a time as this, where our testimony would become our shining glory for your kingdom. Break us free so we can be used to help set others free forever and ever, in Jesus's name. I love you so much. Thank you for being my Heavenly father and never letting me go—never letting us go. In Jesus's name I pray, amen and amen.*

This is the beginning of my story to *true breakthrough*, and I pray that from this, *you will never be the same.*

From the beginning, God embraced me through the struggle of being born with clubfoot on both feet. My parents fought for me as they listened closely to the voice of the Lord for what to do concerning my special feet. At that time, they knew there was a calling on my life, but they didn't know how huge it was—nor did they quite understand it. But they accepted it and walked with me through it one day, week, month, and year at a time.

In the midst of this, I was always considered so different, and at times, some would say *weird* because I kept to myself and didn't speak much to anyone. I remained attached to my mommy every step of the way. I had so much *love* around me but always felt so alone and misunderstood from this special thing called "God's anointing." I knew I belonged somewhere but never quite knew where or with whom I would ever feel like I was more than enough—or even enough at all. A fire burned on the inside of me that caused me to know I was set apart for a reason. To what extent, I didn't know. The cost of it all was a blur...

So what did I do? I fell in love with Jesus; the one who every day made sure I knew I mattered no matter what. The one who let me know I was everything to him because of his unconditional, unfailing, and never-ending love. My mother did a great job of this also, but I still knew there were expectations that naturally came with being their baby daughter. At that time, I began to live my life as a people-pleaser, so the acceptance would come; the expectations would be fulfilled, and then I could be seen as a human being instead of an invisible, different/weird but anointed little girl.

Sometimes, as many of us know, being chosen has a cost. It may cost you friends and relationships, and it may bring you lonely seasons, many spiritual attacks (for reasons unknown), and a journey from "Pain to Purpose." (*Pain to Purpose* is the title of a powerful book written by my auntie, Pastor Charlyn Michelle Singleton.) From a young age, I began to live like I had to prove myself to anyone and everyone who came into my life, and I would go above and beyond just to make sure people knew they mattered just for who they were because I had never felt like I did.

I began to love and trust everyone who came into my reach, holding onto them with all my might, because I always felt I would lose them once they realized I was different: anointed, called, chosen, and destined by God. It felt like a curse within a blessing because all I wanted was what I constantly gave to all those around me: acceptance, understanding, and unconditional *love.* I was not holding on to the fact that God had already given me that and more.

I spent most of my life living in this lie, searching for what I already had but not allowing Jesus to be more than enough...do you get it now? I wanted from others what God desired from me. He allowed me to feel what he felt until a year ago, when we sat in each other's presence, and he spoke to the depths of my heart, soul, and spirit. God said to me: "When will I become more than enough for you? This whole time, you have always been more than enough for me!"

I have always had an amazing family: my poppy, who always made sure we had more than enough and provided above and beyond what I have ever known any man to provide for his family. And along with being a pastor at Loveland Church and a boss at Edison, he never missed a beat. He was at every track meet, volleyball game, basketball game, dance performance/competition, and sports game to see me cheer. I still don't know how he did it.

My mommy…wow. Words can't express the power of her anointing and her straight-to-heaven's-heart-prayers. She stood with me, by me, and for me, even when I didn't have much of a fight left. I had everything I needed and wanted without even asking, and she shared my tears, joys, heartbreaks, mess-ups, triumphs, over-comings, and most of all, my joy. Through God, she is why I am who I am becoming today and each day I wake.

My two sisters stood with me and fought for me (literally), and I did the same for them. Our love for each other goes undefined because it's just that powerful—in our hearts and in our tears. All my grandparents…I am and always have been loved beyond measure and held sacredly for my arrival time into destiny with their protection, wisdom, and prayers. As you're reading this, you might be thinking: So what's the problem?

The problem was me knowing deep down inside; at times through conversations and just even within myself that I, Reyna Joy Banks, had to make it. I didn't want to mess up or let anyone down, especially God. When I was born with clubfoot on both feet and had casts on my feet from three months until I was three and a half years old (my parents were praying over my feet day and night), we had come to realize something. We knew that God had called me and chosen me for something so huge. He needed me to have a personal encounter with him from birth so that I would always know to whom I belonged and with whom I was going to fulfill a life of destiny.

I realized I was called to be a part of bringing his kingdom in Heaven to his kingdom on Earth. This has kept me humble throughout my entire life because I know what it means to be nothing without Jesus. In all of this, the enemy tried to silence me by the feeling of never being enough, always having to prove myself, people-pleasing, and living up to expectations of others—especially myself. It's a dangerous road living with that weight, but thank God for grace and mercy! His grace and mercy kept me over and over again.

I will continue my story throughout this journey, but it's just to remind you that you are not alone, and it is your time to be *bold, beautiful,* and *blessed!* Let's continue in our steps to *true breakthrough.*

Step 2: *Unfailing Love* from *God*

True breakthrough comes when you begin to understand the *unfailing love* God has for you. It's a love that endlessly loves. It's a love you can't earn or gain. As a matter of fact, it's a love that has no single definition; it's hard to completely describe or define it. It's a father as he looks at his child being born type of love. It's a mother giving birth to her first child type of love. It's a person being healed of cancer kind of love. It's a blind man being able to see type of love. It's a woman being healed from thirty years of bleeding type of love. It's a child being brought to life after dying type of love. It's a creator speaking, and this whole world coming into fruition type of love. It's our God sending his one and only son to Earth to live and die just for us to be reconnected to him again type of love. It is a love that doesn't need an explanation or reconciliation; it is as God is, and it will always be forever and for eternity.

> For God so loved the world, that he gave his only begotten son, that whosoever believeth in him should not perish, but have everlasting life. (John 3:16, KJV)

Step 3: *Victory* over *Everything*

You have to constantly remember and renew your mind in the fact that you are the *victor* and not the *victim.* How can we take on the role of the victim when Jesus paid it all at the Cross for you and for me? You are always the victor because he has already won, and we are just a part of the manifestation of the ultimate win here on Earth.

It's easy to take the blame and throw a pity party, but what's easier is to take back your joy and praise God for the struggle to something greater and even better. It's called: *fulfilling your God-Ordained destiny*.

For example: a plié in dance is a balletic movement that means to bend. In almost every step or ballet sequence, you must plié in order to rise or to leap. So to go up, you have to have a moment to bend, go to a downward position, and prep for your greatest jump/leap that is only made beautiful from the plié taken before you soar into the air. You see now? Dance with your Heavenly father instead of trying to dance alone and forgetting to go down at his appointed time. Rise at his appointed time for your life: your story.

Stop and Journal

#DAY5
#TRUEBREAKTHROUGH

"Let your eyes look straight ahead, fix your gaze directly before you.
Make level paths for your feet and take only ways that are firm."
(Proverbs 4:25-26 NIV)

JOURNAL #9:

What will you choose?
Why?

1. Transparency or being numb?

2. Unfailing love or limited love?

3. Victory or victim?

True breakthrough comes from you making up your mind and submitting it to your spirit, aligning your body so your heart is positioned to choose to be the head and not the tail; to say "it is well" and release a word into the depths of your soul. Then you can speak out loud to the world and say, "I am whole, healed, and free in Jesus's name. Amen!"

Will you choose to be free? I say *yes*! Why? Because you wouldn't have picked up this book if you weren't tired of being weighed down by who you were…six years ago, one year ago, or even three months ago.

You are more than *the you* you were then, and you can choose to be more than *the you* that you were yesterday. God loves you, his son endured the Cross for you, and his greatest gift to you is his love and his Spirit within you.

Stop and Journal

JOURNAL #10: (write quote here)

Will you love you enough to learn the love of your Creator?

DAY 6

Power in Patience

Be still and know that I am God.

—Psalms 46:10 (NIV)

Day 6 is living in the true essence of the "Power in Patience." After a true breakthrough, the healing comes in steps and different phases. You cannot and will not get a true breakthrough by these three steps in one day. It takes time, and the process must come full circle in order for you to be whole, healed, and free.

The power in patience doesn't mean sitting and waiting, nor does it mean being stagnant as you wait for the true you to be free. It means proactively waiting on the birthing of the *new you* that can't co-exist with the *old you*. It means that each day you wake, you are standing in the fullness and knowledge that there is a greater you to spring forth. But you can't do so until you stand in the power of moving forward patiently as your healing, wholeness, and freedom to fly comes into play and fruition.

You must begin to understand that you don't belong to yourself and never did. You have always belonged to someone so much greater, who literally holds the whole world in his hands. There's power in patience; all that you are called to be and do takes time. It's something that can't be rushed or forced but simply lived in a moment of time, until you wake up each day, knowing that waking up *today* was for something so much greater than yourself.

> But those who wait upon the Lord shall renew
> their strength, they shall mount up with wings

like eagles, they shall run and not be weary, they
shall walk and not faint. (Isaiah 40:31, NKJV)

The Three Points:

1. Transparency
2. Unfailing Love
3. Victory

These three focus points will keep cycling through in each
moment and season of your life. Your transitions will be tested, and
you will be extremely vulnerable—but only to God—not others.
With people, you will be guarded and at times, completely misunderstood, but the beauty of it is that you are going to begin to matter
to *you*, just the way you matter to God. And what others feel about
you will start to matter less and less than ever before. The things
that people placed upon you and labeled you as will begin to fall off
because naturally, you will start to walk in the fullness of who God
says you are and has called you to be.

At times, we fall into the shadows of every word spoken over or
upon us—words that never belonged to us to begin with. Words like:
fake, conceited, selfish, ugly, too dark, too light, too tall, too short,
too thick, too skinny, ghetto, oreo, fat, too pretty, bossy, too quiet,
too nice, talks to much, too joyful, bad attitude, and too preachy. Or
even these phrases: "She thinks she's all that," and "She thinks she's
perfect!" We will tackle that last one in just a little bit; it was my
greatest enemy for far too long.

Take a moment and think about the words that have shaped
you throughout your entire life. Think about how they may have
possibly caused you to be less than the amazing woman that you are,
for God first, for yourself second, and then for the beautiful people attached to your journey third. This is the moment you become
transparent with yourself and *speak the whole truth*, and nothing but
the truth so help and save your destiny!

Speak the words and write them down. Tear the paper out of
your journal once you are finished pouring out every single desti-

ny-threatening word that was placed upon you not by your choice. Then speak these exact words: "I rebuke these words that the enemy used to place restrictions on me and my destiny, in Jesus's name. And as I rip this paper up to pieces, I speak in the name of Jesus Christ. It is done, it is well, and it is finished. Amen."

Faithfulness takes *patience* in holding out for the *good* that *God* has promised you, and through *perseverance,* you grow into *wisdom* that helps you hold onto the good that *God* places in your hands. In the midst of it all, stay in it simply because you are worth it.

You must now know that every word ever spoken over you that was misaligned with your identity no longer exists. In this very moment, the Lord is saying to my spirit, "It is over, beloved, and it is no longer a part of your present or future. What once was isn't anymore, and through *patience,* I will birth your *power* through your testimony to overcome what had you bound. Through this, by *faith,* you allowed me to *break* each and every single *chain.* It is done, it is well, and it is finished. 'By my stripes you are healed' (Isaiah 53:4–5, KJV). Amen!"

What if your greatest awakening moment is just after your season of being *patient* without worry and stepping into the *endurance* of being all that God says you are? See, *becoming* is a part of the requirement to step into the next place of position. You have to be willing to be developed, purged, released, restored, kept, tucked away, and ready to share your testimony. What is life without being stretched? What is life without being prepared? What is life without going from glory to glory to glory—not just in destiny, but in your *faith?*

Your *"Power in Patience"* is life or death for so many, including the hearts you haven't even come into contact with just yet. Some people can only be brought forth to press you in until you are positioned fearlessly in that perfect appointed moment. But you can miss it if patience isn't a part of your character and way of life. What will be your testimony and legacy? Being where you're supposed to be when you're supposed to be there to touch another soul, or being everywhere because your lack of patience causes you to doubt the hand of God concerning the destiny he has perfectly sketched out and painted for you? What are you willing to let go of in order to receive what he has for you, for his glory?

```
Quest For Enlightenment

Faithfulness——————>Wisdom

Perseverance

Patience              Endurance
Holding out           Holding onto
for good              the good

By: Sarah Catherine Walker
```

My Greatest Test Yet in This: My Testimony

Sometimes, your *"Power in Patience"* is staying a little longer than you want to at a certain place, going where you don't want to go, and dealing with what you don't want to deal with. It can even be finishing what you've started.

I was one of the victims of the Target Scandal a few years ago and hackers wiped out my account. At first, I was in denial. My mom had mentioned it to me, and I immediately stated, "I'm not affected by that, in Jesus's name!" But I should've checked my account anyways. Two days went by, and something told me to check my account. Four transactions had already gone through my account from the credit card thefts. By day three, there were multiple transactions, and I rushed to my bank with smoke practically steaming from my head—like a cartoon character. But God's sweet, still, small voice was saying, "Peace, be still, be still, my daughter."

I took a deep breath and walked into the bank in peace and faith, knowing that God was going to handle everything for me. I explained what was going on to a banker, and she told me to have a seat. After waiting for forty-five minutes, I was getting ready to walk out and head to another bank, but God spoke and said, "Wait! Have patience, my daughter!" So I sat there and waited fifteen more minutes. Finally, the most joyful, tiny woman came over to me and asked, "Have you been helped?"

I informed her I hadn't been helped at all, and I told her I had been hit badly by the Target Scandal. She said, "Oh, my goodness. Come with me, please!" Immediately, she pulled up my account, contacted the theft department and began to go through and highlight all of the transactions that weren't mine. Then she asked me, "How are you so calm and peaceful about this?"

I stated, "Because I know that God has it in his hands, and it's going to be okay! Why be angry about something I don't have control over?"

"Wow, your faith is amazing to see. Are you a Christian?" she asked.

I said, "Yes, I am. But more than that, I love Jesus and have a personal relationship with him."

"I need that. I want that in my life, too. How do I get Jesus in my life and not become saddened by the things in this world and my own situations? What do I have to do to have Jesus in my life and be at peace? I want to be happy again. I haven't been happy in a very long time!" she said to me.

I told her, "All you have to do is do exactly what you just did: profess it and confess it with your words and your heart. He hears you, and he loves you so much. He wouldn't have allowed me to be here if he wasn't drawing you closer to him. It starts with talking to him, just like you're talking to me. That's what prayer is. Then read his living Word, the Holy Bible. I can send you scriptures once a week, or each day, for you to read and study so you can begin to experience the fullness of his love for you. Your best days are ahead, and he is proud of you."

She started to cry and received every single word that came out of my mouth, explaining it was all a confirmation from a pastor from the week before. She realized God's love for her like never before and saw how he was calling her into his presence for an even greater purpose.

As I cried with her, I told her to study the story of Hannah in the Bible, along with the daily scriptures I would send her. Then I mentioned to her that I was glad I didn't leave from being impatient.

I was actually happy that someone had hacked my account so I could meet her and introduce her to the love of Jesus that was ever so present in that three-hour ordeal. We were both so blessed and realized it's so true what the Word of God says:

> All things work together for the good of those who love God and are called according to His purpose. (Romans 8:28, NIV)

What have you lost your *"Power in Patience"* in? When you think back, you realize there was a defining moment in that space that you possibly missed. It was all due to not understanding the shift and full purpose of why God had positioned you there when he did.

So now, let's break down the true meaning of *"Power In Patience."* What does that really mean, and what does that look like?

Power: the ability to do something or act in particular way, especially as a faculty or quality. (Google definition)

In: used to indicate limitation or qualification, as of situation, condition, relation, manner, action, etc. (Dictionary.com)

Patience: the capacity to accept or tolerate delay, trouble, or suffering without getting angry or upset. (Google definition)

So, in sum *"Power In Patience"* means: "The ability to indicate qualification to accept delay or suffer without getting upset."

Read that one more time and take it in. This time, as you make it personal, in this very present moment, ask yourself: *What does that mean to me?* Then journal it.

For me, it confirmed what God had been speaking to my spirit while I'd been on the same journey: "Just be!" There is so much power in that alone. When you learn how to just *be,* you're telling God that you trust his process to your progress into becoming your absolute best! I can't speak on or write about what I don't know, and I can't speak or write what God hasn't spoken to the depths of my spirit, heart, and soul. Timing is everything, and in his time, your defining moments will come to pass. But you must surpass the bounds and chains of anger and frustration when things don't quite go the way you expect them to.

"Who can you trust more?" is what I had to ask myself. And I answered, "The one who created everything from nothing and turned it into something so beautiful and life-changing. It's what we see each day we wake. He spoke, and things were manifested, so how could I insult God or myself by thinking I can trust myself over the ultimate creator? I can't, so I choose to trust him." The moment you surrender and submit, the more you will gain "power in patience."

Stop and Journal

#DAY6
#POWERINPATIENCE

"Be still and know that I am God."
(Psalm 46:10 NIV)

In totality, "power in patience" means:
"The ability to indicate qualification to accept
delay or suffering without getting upset."

JOURNAL #11:

1. **Write down three main areas in which you need to work on having patience:**

A.

B.

C.

2. *Write down three main reasons why you have been weak in patience in those areas.*

A.

B.

C.

3. *Write down three ways you are going to work on having "power in patience:"*

A.

B.

C.

At the end of your journaling, seal it with this:
It is done, it is well and it is finished.
In Jesus' name, amen!

DAY 7

The Attack of Your Joy

The joy of the Lord is my strength.

—Nehemiah 8:10 (NIV)

Day 7 is possibly heartbreaking. Why? It's the day that someone perhaps did all they could to take you off course. It's the day when something may be stirred up on the inside of you that you felt died a long time ago, or even died after you completed day two. There is one thing I have to explain to you that was explained to me years ago. It is never the person himself or herself attacking you. In some way, people are always being used by another force or spirit through a door they somehow opened in order for it to come in and come against you. This is similar to a very important part of the Job story in the Bible. Job is well known for his sufferings and his restoration, but the most critical part of this story takes place in Job 2–26.

Job's dearest friends Eliphaz, Bildad, and Zophar came to visit him and comfort him, so it seemed, but with their words and lack of submission to the Holy Spirit, they each challenged Job in a way that was outside the will of God. As mentioned in Job 22, Eliphaz openly tried to get Job to repent with the wrong motives, which was what Satan was trying to prove and accuse Job of, knowing that wasn't Job's character or his way of living.

In my study Bible, it breaks down the mistake Eliphaz made in Job 22:21–30 "Thereby good shall come unto thee…" In persuading Job to repent so he could recover his health and prosperity, Eliphaz was unintentionally siding with Satan in his accusations against Job and God. Earlier, Satan had accused Job of serving God for what God could do for him (1:9–11). Understand that if Job were to repent for a sin never done so he could gain God's blessing, he could have very well, at that very moment, been accused of serving God simply for his personal gain. Even though the words of Eliphaz express the importance of repentance eloquently, they were spoken with impure motives. There wasn't a hint of sympathy in his heart for the suffering Job.

As you take time to read this story for yourselves, you will see how spirits that are not of God wait for an open door in order to use people in such a way that almost destroys the true essence of who you are. Remember: it isn't the person. It's an unconfined demonic spirit that is using them to take you off course. The ultimate goal is to distract you and keep you from your destiny in a crucial way. If you don't believe me, then think about this...

Every time you get in a good space and step into something new that you know God called you to, something happens to throw you off course. It could be an argument, someone's jealousy, attitudes, work, family, pre-judgment, or assumptions from others. All of these things are considered a spirit and not a godly one. They are on assignment to destroy the greatest thing that God could've ever given you. It's your voice in this world, through your gifts and talents, all in alignment with your God-Given destiny.

Spiritual warfare is something that is too often ignored or tolerated so that no one has to deal with it face to face. But it is as real as your name, and the assignment of Satan's kingdom is to destroy everything and anything that God has given you in order to help expand his kingdom here on Earth. (1 Peter 5:7–9) Every time you hit another landmark and defining moment in your life, *the attack of your joy* will come head on. It will continue until they are done keeping you from your greater calling in and out of season.

Someone once told me, "The enemy and his demons never take a break, so why should we" (Pastor Bill Dancey, member of Loveland Church)? This was a pivotal moment and revelation in my life; because in that season when that word was revealed to me, I was living my life on an emotional rollercoaster that only God and my spiritual mom, "Turtledove" Mom Brewington, could help save me from. The thing that had me damaged the most was that it was a part of my make-up, meaning: I didn't know any other way to live but to be consistently up and down, crying and cheering, angry and happy, anxious and persevering. I was a mess, and I didn't know there was any other way to exist, except in that emotional state.

What I came to realize was that it wasn't me, and I wasn't the problem; the spirits that were being used to oppress my destiny and my presence were the actual problem. Those nights when your sleep is affected; your dreams are a disturbance, and *rest* no longer exists… those are the nights that you must know you are truly on the right track with destiny.

"Why?" you may ask.

I want to share with you what I have come to realize throughout my life. What threat are you when you are in alignment with the options of the enemy and out of alignment with the humble but yet profound and world-changing will of your Heavenly father? That could be your answer; it was definitely mine. I recognized throughout my life and the lives of thousands around me, that the enemy doesn't seem to attack when you are out of the will of God for your destiny. It's when you *are* walking in the will and calling of God for your destiny when the war starts.

It's the same thing with people who come against you in your day-to-day life. When you are doing and living the exact same type of life as they are and not standing out and being a part of the change, they are for you and cool with you. Then when you start standing out, making a difference, walking, talking, living, and pressing into destiny like you were always *chosen* to, the jealousy, hate, conflict, strife, animosity, deception, and attacks rise against you stronger than ever. This is what I—and many others—have experienced and observed. The key to all of this is to not allow yourself to become a part of the insecurity issues but to show them how to love themselves through the love of Christ.

You might be saying, "Are you nuts? You're joking, right? For what? Why do I have to be the bigger person?" And I say, "Because if you won't, who will? If you don't show them the love of Christ, who will?" Take yourself out of the place of offense and step into the place of: *where is this coming from, and who hurt them in order for them to feel okay with hurting me?*

> And herein do I exercise myself, to have always a conscience void of offense toward God, and toward men. (Acts 24:16, NKJV)

Now you get it, right? That's what I had to digest, and boy, was it a hard one to swallow. I had been treated so bad for so long by so many people who I hadn't done anything to. In the midst of it all, God taught me how to *love* them past their actions and hate. He also taught me how to war against the enemy in such a mighty way, I no longer saw the people coming against me. Instead, I began to open my spiritual eyes and see what was really using them.

The Spirit of Offense

Being on the offense is a dangerous way to live your life and or even dwell in for one second. It keeps you bound to the past and the furthest away from fulfilling your *destiny.* "Offense" as defined by Google.com: "annoyance or resentment brought about by a perceived insult to or disregard for oneself or one's standards or principles." One of the many times offense is mentioned in the Bible, it says, "A brother offended is harder to be won than a strong city: and their contentions are like the bars of a castle" (Proverbs 18:19, NKJ). It's how the enemy gets us to limit the hand of God in our lives without even sinning. No one and nothing is ever worth the progression of your destiny, so I challenge you to *let it go!*

Stop and Journal

#DAY7
#THEATTACKOFYOURJOY

"The joy of the Lord is my strength."
(Nehemiah 8:10 NIV)

JOURNAL #12:

1. What am I still holding on to that has caused me to limit the hand of God, due to the spirit of offense?

2. Who brought offense into my life, and through what circumstances?

3. How can I begin to let go, one day at a time?

Now, give it to God before you step into Day Eight.

DAY 8

The Fight

The Lord shall fight for you and you shall hold your peace.
—Exodus 14:14 (NKJV)

Day 8 consists of the first *real fight of your life*. From day one to day seven, I'd had enough and couldn't take it much longer. First of all, having to go back to all the things that, yes helped make me into the woman I am today, but also wounded and broke me beyond words, was torture. And so far, I have only touched the surface.

> Hath the Lord have great delight in burnt offerings and sacrifices, as in obeying the voice of the Lord? Behold, to obey is better than to sacrifice. (1 Samuel 15:22, NKJV)

#*Transparency*Moment

I was so tired of being broken, so tired of my joy and love for people being taken advantage of…so tired of feeling like I was never enough because my anointing was misunderstood. I was so tired of the complexities of not being "Black enough" or not being "light enough," but to God, I was one of his greatest lights, still so brightly lit from what he had told me, all for his glory. But at that point in my life, I didn't care. I wanted people to accept me for me and allow me to be free to be myself.

I was dying, just trying to live as the Reyna who God had always intended me to be. I had never felt like I mattered unless I did something amazing or perfect. And then, after that, I still felt like I wasn't enough for family, friends, boyfriends, the Church, being a pastor's daughter, an athlete, dancer, in the limelight, a leader, speaker, teacher, student, and more. I was dying, and all I wanted to do was live.

I became angry that I made my actions based off of my decision to try to please so many people. I lived like God wasn't enough or doing enough on my behalf, when he had done and was doing more than enough already. I allowed people to make me angry with God for giving me his heart when it was continually walked all over. My joy was constantly taken from me, and I grew weary in well-doing to a great capacity. I was constantly carrying around "baby Reyna Joy" on my back, when I realized that I had to let her go so I could live again—live like never before—before it was too late. There were three very pivotal moments in my life that awakened me to the spiritual weight I had been carrying from such a young age.

I had thoughts about no longer wanting to dwell on earth because of the fight to just be me. These thoughts then became actions during my three suicide attempts that were detrimental to the Kingdom of God, but he kept me every time. He sent angels that showed me *the me* in the future, helping change the world for God's glory. Two of God's most well-known angels, Gabriel and Michael, were released to visit me a few times to cover, protect, and bring me peace during these pivotal seasons in destiny, along with many others. It wasn't until early spring of 2013 when this book was first placed in my spirit by God, that the archangel came and took dominion over my home while I went away to dance in Denver, Colorado. There was a spiritual war that was declared as soon as I walked out of my home and locked the door.

Let me explain: just as we see things in the *natural,* every single day, we do certain things repetitiously that define our set schedule. In the *spiritual* realm, there are identical, repetitious, and continuous things that transpire in order to *protect* us or *destroy* us. God's whole kingdom is at work, and all of heaven is backing up you and me. So in knowing this, understand that we have a choice. I have a choice, and you have a choice, to stand in faith or surrender to fear.

The Fight

1. Sometimes, it's you not doing a thing and instead resting in Christ as he sends out his angels to war on your behalf.
2. Sometimes, it's calling your angels forth to go hard on your behalf.
3. Sometimes, it's falling on your face or knees and speaking in your holy language to your Heavenly father as you war and denounce everything that is trying to destroy you.

For me, it was resting and not fighting it in my own strength and allowing God to be God and reign over my entire situation. I'm not perfect, but it felt so good when I surrendered and acknowledged that what God was requiring of me wasn't what the world would usually require of us. He wanted me to sleep while his kingdom fought. Think about it…he loves us so much that he says, "You sleep and rest in me so my Kingdom can come to Earth concerning you, my beloved!" That moment changed my life forever, and I haven't been the same since.

Stop and Journal

#DAY8
#THEFIGHT

"The Lord shall fight for you and you shall hold your peace."
(Exodus 14:14 NKJV)

JOURNAL #13:

1. "Is this my fighting season?"

2. "Is this my resting season?"

3. "Is this my warring season?"

4. "Is this my surrender season?"

> "Give thanks to the LORD, for he is good.
> His love endures forever.
> Give thanks to the God of gods.
> His love endures forever.
> Give thanks to the Lord of lords:
> His love endures forever."
> (Psalm 136:1-3 NIV)

When you truly seek God and hear the answer to these questions, what will you do? I challenge you to take your time. Don't move on to day nine until you know the answers. When you believe you have received the answers to the questions in the journal, you can then begin to submit to God's calling over your life, in every season to come. What I learned during my journey is that the greatest fight of my life is in my resting place, where I am untouchable from the world as God shows me what His love looks like, fights like, sounds like, feels like, and wins like. Just as he has done for me, he is going to do the same for you.

> Give thanks to the Lord, for He is Good.
> His love endures forever.
> Give thanks to the God of gods.
> His love endures forever.
> Give thanks to the Lord of lords.
> His love endures forever. (Psalms 136:1–3, NIV)

DAY 9

Fear Unconfined

*Fear: an unpleasant emotion caused by the belief that someone
or something is dangerous, likely to cause pain, or a threat
Unconfined: not confined to a limited space
(definitions from Google.com)*

Day 9 is gearing toward the woman who is a bit opposite
from the last chapter and has chosen to be silent and not
fight at all, let alone express what's really going on. *Fear
Unconfined* is a dangerous place to live, especially when you have
a destiny for your life. At times, we choose to live in a place of *fear*
rather than *faith* because it takes more fight to step up and step out,
instead of staying right where you are, allowing the enemy to keep
you from the greatest *you* there could ever be.

I think and I believe I hit a nerve here. Okay, so here is the deal:

1. Do you want your life back?
2. Do you want to start living again?
3. Do you have enough fear that you will die without taking
   the chance to actually live and affect at least one life?
4. If you answered yes to the above questions, what are you
   going to do about it?

You have come too far to be held back by what is keeping you
from your destiny and promises. Let's be honest: What do you have
to lose? If you want your life back, then you have to surrender to
the fact that the battle is not yours; it's the Lord's. That is his prom-

ise, and it's your promise; because the moment that you came into this world, you came forth with greatness stamped on your heart and your life by God and God alone. If you aren't experiencing the greatness, then there is a blockage in the tunnel of your ordained grace, favor, and overflow of God's anointing power that dwells on the inside of you.

> For God has not given us the spirit of fear but of power and of love and of a sound mind. (2 Timothy 1:7, NKJV)

1. Do you want your life back?

This is the first step you take in order to begin this process before moving forward to day ten.

    a) Speak life into yourself: Tell yourself you can do everything that fear has been telling you (and tells you daily), you can't do. Begin to write it all down and command your mind to submit to your heart. Then tell both your mind and your heart to submit to your spirit, which is of the Holy Spirit.

    b) Change your way of living by living in wisdom rather than carelessness; in increase rather than lack; in peace instead of chaos; in joy and not sorrow; in faith instead of fear.

    c) Choose to speak life and not death, at all times, even when you don't feel as alive or prepared. Oftentimes, you are your only enemy. Why self-sabotage your destiny when you rightfully deserve what you have been promised?

> You frame your world with the words that come out of your mouth each and every single day. (Pastor Touré Roberts)

2. Do you want to start living again?

Go back and remember what you overcame on day one through day eight. Close your eyes, take a deep breath, and whisper to your heart, "The victory has already been won. I've come this far; it's time to finish this race and overcome so I can begin to live again!"

a) You must believe that it's in you to *live* and not *die,* go where you've never gone before, and do what you have never done—whatever that is and whatever that looks like…

For example, I had always wanted to go kayaking, and I was in a season of my life when I was losing the joy of why I was still here and pressing past what told me *no* every single day. I needed something to keep me in a place of peace and understanding as I went forth through the refining season. So I went to a coupon site and searched "water sports." Guess what popped up? Kayaking for a huge discount for two hours! Something told me to buy a double kayak. I wasn't quite sure why I would do that when it was just me, but I was obedient and bought the double.

Later, that same day, one of the girls I mentor came to me, broken from a relationship that was tainting her joy and presence as a whole. She couldn't keep the tears from falling and didn't have hope left; she wanted to end her life due to some *boy.* I say "boy" because a real man speaks life, not death, at all times. This boy was breaking her down with his words until she had nothing left on the inside of her to live for. I told her I would walk with her through it as God led me and guided me to help her toward her ultimate healing. I mentioned my kayaking excursion, and she wanted to go but explained her lack of finances. I told her, "It's already been paid for!"

She became so excited and her tears of sorrow instantly became tears of joy because it was as simple as someone hearing her cry and tending to her pain. When we went kayaking that weekend, it changed both of our lives in a very strange way. Who would have thought that kayaking could restore so much in just two hours?

My friend was given a second wind by God and knew that he heard her, saw her, honored her, cherished her, and loved her, no matter how many times her actions showed the lack of love that she had for herself. That day and week, he taught her how to *love* herself beyond a love she never knew before. I realized why I had *to live* and not *die*... Someone's future could depend on your presence and obedience to God.

The price for her restoration was already paid for. It wasn't just through the kayaking trip but through God hearing her cry, even before she was formed in her mother's womb. It was in him already knowing that this day would come, where she had to die to her past in order to live like never before, in Jesus.

b) The next step is leaving it all behind, even if that means a person or thing you've always felt you've needed the most. A perfect example of this step is when you are in a serious relationship with a man. For instance, if the man you are currently with is not your husband, and you feel like you haven't mattered since who knows when or maybe never, then *let it go*! In another instance, there may be something that you go to in order to just feel okay, or to get through another day. But it doesn't do anything for your destiny. It actually kills your destiny off, one inch at a time, and you need to *let it go*!

c) Finally, you must realize *who you are* and *whose you are*. Think about that for a second. Knowing and understanding who you are, are the main factors to really, truly living again. What that means and what that looks like is totally up to you. There isn't one book in the world that can tell you the answer to this, except the true and living Word of God. The *Bible* brings God's love for you, and the destiny assigned to you, to life.

d) Everything I'm saying and explaining is exactly what I had to experience during my *30-Day Journey to Loving the Woman in Me*. Even when I wanted to say *no*, I fought for my *yes* because I knew that my *no* could and would cost me nearly everything. I wasn't willing to allow someone else to die because I didn't want to fight to see myself through God's eyes.

3. Do you have enough fear to be afraid that you will die, never having taken the chance to actually live and affect at least one life?

Say this: "Hello, fear! You can't stay here anymore; you've actually been here too long. I am worth more than what you are allowing me to see, for when I see myself through God's eyes, there's a completely different me who is called to arise. I see you are afraid. I will do what's never been done before and begin to change this nation and world with one awakening moment at a time. I decree, with each breath I take, that with God, I will touch many souls each day I wake. Be very afraid because I am no longer going to be held captive by you or *the me* I was before today."

"As I take this *30-Day Journey to Loving the Woman in Me,* I will not allow you to take what rightfully belongs to me. You have kept me handcuffed for far too long. I am a champion. I am a woman of honor and power who is not to be shaken. I am equipped for the greatness being birthed deep down inside of me. I am not yours anymore; I am the Lord's and am fearfully and wonderfully made *for his glory,* to bring his kingdom in Heaven to Earth. So goodbye, fear. Hello, faith. I am a firm believer that in this very moment, my best days are ahead."

"In Jesus's name, I decree and declare that I shall live in faith and never to be the same. I am worth believing in and am pressing toward the mark because my promises are awaiting my arrival. So in this moment right now, I will say I am alive and beginning to live as *the me* I was always created to be, fearlessly! Amen."

4. What are you to do about it?

You just do it!

Stop and Journal

#DAY9
#FEARUNCONFINED

Fear: an unpleasant emotion caused by the belief that someone or something is dangerous, likely to cause pain, or a threat

Uncontained: not confined to a limited space

(Google definitions of "fear" and "uncontained")

JOURNAL #14:

Write your faith declaration to God and the new you:

Now, rest!

DAY 10

Searching

Ask, and it shall be given you; seek,
and ye shall find; knock, and it shall be opened unto you.

—Matthew 7:7, KJV

D ay 10 is defined by the *search*. During your process of all the days leading up to this special day, you have been purging your system from the things that were keeping you and hindering you from becoming and being the *whole, healed,* and *free* you. *The Search* is: what does this look like, feel like, sound like, move like, and speak like? It's the ultimate search in you seeing *the defined you* in destiny and purpose, limitlessly, without question, fear, or doubt.

> I can do all things through Christ Jesus who strengthens me. (Philippians 4:13, KJV)

You have been so used to being *the you* who was living at the beginning of day nine, and now that you have *rebuked fear* and stepped into *unwavering faith,* there is a transition that occurs, which is defined by *searching* for the new, redefined, limitless you in faith— and no longer in fear.

This process starts with certain steps that have to be taken and mastered one day at a time. Pay close attention to the revelation concerning *the you* who must come forth and no longer be hidden in the crowd or behind the curtain. God does a finishing work, and many things we start we must finish because the journey in finishing it is what's used to purify us. So let's focus on what this process is and what the steps are:

It starts with your quiet time, which is that secret place we talked about at the beginning of this journey. For me, it took a little more searching and seeking than it may take some of you. Why? I lived so much of my life in the people-pleasing mode that I didn't quite know who I was at all outside of people's expectations, opinions, desires, and limitations that they had continually placed on me. So my search was deeper, longer, and took a lot more shaking.

Take the time to understand where you were so you can get the fullness of where you are now and where you are about to go. I had to grab ahold of this and felt so full because I realized that the more I had been through, the greater the story, and the more lives I could touch. Understand the depths of your past and present, and through that, you will begin to comprehend at least one fourth of the capacity of your bold and beautiful future! Let me show you how...

Stop and Journal

#DAY10
#SEARCHING

"Ask, and it shall be given you; seek, and ye shall
find; knock, and it shall be opened unto you."
(Matthew 7:7 KJV)

JOURNAL #15: (Write these down)

A. Who were you?

1. People-pleaser
2. Taker, not a giver
3. Pride kept you from receiving
4. Never enough

5. Felt entitled
6. Misunderstood
7. A failure (in your own thoughts)

Choose one of the seven and circle it!

Next, read the story of Mary and Elizabeth in Luke 1:39-45.

"But as it is written, eye hath not seen, nor ear heard,
neither have entered into the heart of man, the things
which God hath prepared for them that love him."
(1 Corinthians 2:9 KJV)

You may still be asking yourself: Why do I have to go back and do this? You must fully begin to understand where you were in order to know where you are now. Then the transition into who you have to become for where you are going will sustain you. It's in you, and now it's time to bring it out of yourself, beloved. Tap in and begin to *be* so you can *become*...so you will already *be*. There is only one you with a purpose that only God himself can give to you.

Now, in this time, God is going to reveal to you who your Elizabeth is because as you and I know, living in your destiny was never meant to be done alone. Stay in your secret place, and she will be revealed. It's birthing time, once we get these next five days of grace defined and realigned in your *now* with God. The second half of your journey will be breathtaking.

Read the story of Mary and Elizabeth in Luke 1:39–45.

But as it is written, Eye hath not seen, nor ear
heard, neither have entered into the heart of
man, the things which God hath prepared for
them that love him. (1 Corinthians 2:9, KJV)

Stop and Journal

JOURNAL #16:

Find a scripture that God has given you on this day, as you were in your secret place on the search: the deepest search of you...

(Define what it means to you and how it relates to your overcoming as you step into the new.)

DAY 11

Realization of What Died

Therefore if any man be in Christ, he is a new creature: old things are passed away; behold, all things are become new.

—2 Corinthians 5:17 (KJV)

On day 11, you begin to step in and step up to the position of preparation in realizing the power that is growing on the inside of you. You have been entrusted with a destiny that only you can birth and that was able to enter when you stepped out of "Day 8: The Fight" and into "Day 9: Fear Unconfined." There was a shift that took place, and in your obedience and your heart simply desiring to be a new and better you, you caused the hand of God to move on your behalf while realizing that *you are ready for the next level.* I mean, you are birthing *something.* You are going into delivery, no longer suppressing the called, chosen, destined, anointed, and groundbreaking you! See, it's already in you from the beginning of time. His Word says: "Before I formed you in your mother's womb, I knew you and I called you to be a prophet upon the nations" (Jeremiah 1:5, KJV).

So you in the spiritual and natural have been positioned to soon give birth to *the you,* God has chosen for such a time as this. Stay in it and stay surrendered with a direct focus. I found myself getting lost right before this point...lost in distractions, trying to save the world, and trying to place expectations on the ones who couldn't deliver what only God could for me. I needed to understand why he had chosen me for something so huge and believe that I was capable of being the one who he manifested it through. Let's be honest: no one is really worthy or has earned the mantle that God has placed upon us or has waiting for us to step into. So we have to get past the fact that in our humanness, there is nothing we can do to change this birthright from God and God alone.

As he told me, I will tell you. The Holy Spirit said to my spirit, "Just embrace yourself! Be bold as you become the greatest woman who only I can manifest in you, through you, and with you for my kingdom as you help me change the world for my glory."

When I mentioned before that we have to die in order to live, I truly meant that. The thing is, in life, certain things can't be birthed until other things have died first. It's been *proven:*

1. *Jacob,* in the Bible, had to leave the places he called home, dying to self each time and leaving things behind that would taint where he and his family were going. Then in obedience to God, he had to return to where his past was, still very much a threat to his present, concerning his older brother Esau and what Jacob had done to him twenty years before. Jacob petitioned God and reminded him of his promises of care and protection in his obedience to returning to his country but also honored and showed gratefulness to God for how far he had brought him and sustained him in purpose and on purpose.

2. *Ruth,* in the Bible, had to die to her past in order to live whole in her present and uncertain future under God's divine order and overflow of favor with Boaz. In the midst of Ruth losing her husband, she died to herself and told Naomi, while still in Moab: "Wither though goest, I will go and where thou lodgest I will lodge: thy people shall be my people, and thy God my God" (Ruth 1:16, KJV).

   It gives a real life portrait of life when it has its struggles and tragedies. Yet it also describes how the faith and faithfulness of godly people caused God to turn tragedy into triumph and defeat into redemption.

3. *Tyler Perry* changed his name from what held him to his past because of the pain his father had caused him. Tyler stepped into who he was always meant to be. His legacy is one that will never die because he knew it took letting go of "Emmitt Perry Jr" in order to become "Tyler Perry." The greater him that we have all come to honor and love for his amazing work in telling profound stories and keeping us in laughter through film, television, and live performance.

All three of these stories have so much substance and truth in the dying process to become the greatest people who only God could have called, chosen, destined, and anointed them while changing their nation and world one day at a time. And while capturing one heart and soul at a time through their gift to love.

There are a number of things that have to die as you are being refined. My "stretching season" consisted of completely letting go of everything and allowing God to be God. I had to understand the depths of Reyna Joy, and the only way to get there, or to even begin to scratch the surface, was to constantly and consistently lay myself at the feet of the Father. It didn't matter if it was at my home, the altar at *One Church International, Loveland Church*, or at my car's steering wheel while parked for hours. Every tear I cried helped me to begin the purging process of the old me. Gradually, I became the purified, solidified, healed, redefined, and chosen Reyna Joy Banks who God had always intended me to be. I "died," and everything attached to who I once was also died. All I began to care about was doing everything for God's glory. And from there, the multiple visions from God that were placed within began to manifest spiritually in the depths of my stomach, and the visions that were once a blur became so clear.

Stop and Journal

#DAY11
#REALIZINGWHATDIED

"Therefore if any man be in Christ, he is a new creature: old things are passed away; behold, all things are become new."

(2 Corinthians 5:17 KJV)

JOURNAL #17:

1. What has God called you to birth?

In the journal, I didn't say, "What do you believe or feel God has called you to birth?" because God is a very direct and precise Father. You know what it is, so this is the step you take to write it down and speak it at the same time. As you do that, every day you wake, you won't be hindered from stepping into the next level of becoming, conceiving, and birthing your God-Ordained destiny.

There was something God taught me years ago when I had moved into my first Hollywood apartment. I was talking to the love of my life at that time, on my move-in day, about the people in my life. I expressed how I wanted them to not just be in my life, but to be a part of it or not in it at all, including him. I was tired of having thousands around me but no one truly and genuinely standing with me and by me. I expressed to him that I had somehow increased a swelling in my life instead of an actual growth—that some things had to fall off and away in order for me to step into who God needed me to be in that season.

That was in 2010, and still to this day, God has had me share that word with many people in the entertainment business, including well-known pastors. Throughout life, it's very easy to have a swelling instead of growth. This means that when you have toxic things and/ or people in your life, a swelling occurs that eventually causes an infection, and in that, you have to allow God to come and clean out the toxins that are suffocating your growth. This is also known as purpose and destiny.

Stop and Journal

JOURNAL #18: Write these definitions down and relate them to people, circumstances, and life.

Toxic:

Swelling:

Infection:

Cleansing:

Versus
Growth:

"I beseech you therefore, brethren, by the mercies of
God, that ye present your bodies a living sacrifice, holy,
acceptable unto God, which is your reasonable service. And
be not conformed to this world: but be ye transformed
by the renewing of your mind, that ye may prove what is
that good, and acceptable, and perfect, will of God."
(Romans 12:1-2 KJV)

I'd rather have one assigned, designed, aligned person in God and of God, standing with me in destiny, than ten who are contrary to my growth and my purpose, causing suffocation and stagnation.
This usually is the final process to dying to self because we don't want to hurt anyone's feelings or step into the fear of being alone. As God recently shared with me, "Are someone's feelings more import-

ant than being obedient to what I am requiring of you to do? Is it more important than my love for you and my direction given to you for you to be aligned with destiny like never before? Love me more than their feelings and your fears by letting them go. In that very moment, I will show them and you, my daughter, what happens when you do destiny with me and for my glory."

> I beseech you therefore, brethren, by the mercies of God, that ye present your bodies a living sacrifice, holy, acceptable unto God, which is your reasonable service, And be not conformed to this world: but be ye transformed by the renewing of your mind, that ye may prove what is that good, and acceptable, and perfect, will of God. (Romans 12:1–2, KJV)

Stop and Journal

JOURNAL #19: (Write these down and speak them out loud.)

1. Three things that were/are causing a swelling in your life:
   A.
   B.
   C.

2. Three elements to what is dying and has already died:
   A.
   B.
   C.

3. Three things that you are finally birthing:
   A.
   B.
   C.

Now, pray and rest.

DAY 12

Wounded but Not Broken

Wounded*: inflict an injury on someone (injure, hurt, harm)*
Broken*: having been fractured or damaged and no longer
in one piece or in working order (www.Google.com)*

Day 12 is when your wounds can no longer break you but begin to build you. This is the breathtaking outcome of what happens when you realize what has died and step into the understanding of: "The movie that God has written and created concerning your life story…" (as my brother, Devon Franklin, states in his book *Produced By Faith).* You have made an executive decision to build off of what was meant to break you.

The questions I had to ask myself (and now I challenge you to do the same) was: What wounds were allowed by God a part of his perfect plan? What wounds were self-inflicted due to going before God and being where he didn't need me to be and going where he didn't want me to go?

What the enemy means for bad, God means for good. And no matter what, all wounds, when dealt with, prepare you for the best seasons of your life. I would not be half or even a quarter of the woman I am today if I didn't go through certain seasons of my life and take on wounds that were possibly meant to kill every inch of me. Every day is a challenge, but I always say, and I will always speak this, "Rejection is God's protection, beloved."

Stop here and turn to Day 12 in your journal and follow the exercises before moving on to the next paragraph.

75

God loves you so much that he chose you to carry out your own story. He knew you could and would allow it to birth the best you to trail blaze for his glory. He allowed many of those things to transpire, all for the day of you living out each fulfilling promise from him. Once the true you is birthed, then the "destiny babies" are birthed all through your *yes* to his *yeses* and *no* to his *nos*.

> According to the eternal purpose which He pur-
> posed in Christ Jesus our Lord: in whom we
> have boldness and access with confidence by
> faith of him. Wherefore I desire that ye faint not
> at my tribulation for you, which is your glory.
> (Ephesians 3:11–13, KJV)

What's so symbolic about this day and chapter is the number of it. Twelve is a very profound number in the Lord, and it's on this day, this hour, this minute, and this second that you are decreeing and declaring your stamp here on Earth. The number twelve means many things, but the most important part of its definition is on www.bible-study.org: "The number twelve is considered a perfect number; it symbolizes God's power and authority, as well as serving as a perfect governmental foundation. It can also symbolize completeness or the nation of Israel as a whole. It's always referred to Jacob and his twelve sons who each represented a tribe of princes." In order to really live out what this is describing, I need you to realize that this day is preparing you for the best season of your life. Knowing and understanding what it is that God says about you is key.

Trust the process.

> Trust in the Lord with all thine heart; and lean
> not unto thine own understanding.
> In all thy ways acknowledge him and he
> shall direct your paths. (Proverbs 3:5–6, KJV)

#DAY12
#WOUNDEDBUTNOTBROKEN

"According to the eternal purpose which He purposed in Christ Jesus our Lord: in whom we have boldness and access with confidence by faith of him. Wherefore I desire that ye faint not at my tribulation for you, which is your glory."
(Ephesians 3:11-13 KJV)

"Rejection is God's protection, beloved."

Stand up, walk to the closest mirror, and as you look at yourself, take a moment to say these exact words:

"Thank you, _____(your name here)_____, for not giving up on me and choosing to overcome. Jesus loves you, and I'm beginning to know what loving you looks like, feels like, and lives like."

In this very moment, many words have healed over without a scab in sight. That's God's love wiping away every blemish that thought it could kill you or keep you from fulfilling your destiny. Yes, yes, yes: it's time to worship, with the understanding that you were chosen for such a journey as this.

"What doesn't kill you can only make you stronger, better, bolder, and greater."

Trust the process…

"Trust in the Lord with all thine heart; and lean not unto thine own understanding. In all thy ways acknowledge him and he shall direct your paths."
(Proverbs 3:5-6 KJV)

DAY 13

It Isn't Your Fault

And we know that all things work together for good to them that
love God, to them who are the called according to His purpose.

—Romans 8:28 (KJV)

On day 13, you might experience backlash. This is because you are at the point of not turning back and instead fully stepping into what was always meant to be. The enemy is always working; it is his full time job to kill, steal, and destroy your joy, peace, hope, faith, and presence as a whole. In knowing this, we have to always be prepared and on guard because as soon as you picked up this book, you became a target to all of Hell. What the enemy didn't realize, however, was that as soon as you picked up this book, you had all of Heaven backing you up. Your best days are ahead.

When you have decided to take a route in life that proclaims you want the best for yourself, there is always an uncomfortable place in and out of season, no matter what anyone has ever said to you or about you. But there is no time lost in Christ. So if it's the attack of being reminded of your past and stepping into the place of: *I've done so much wrong,* you have to bind the spirit of guilt and condemnation in the name of Jesus. Take yourself back from going to that place because the new you who's birthing this new destiny doesn't deserve to be tormented by the past.

Let me take a moment to explain what I had to face in realizing on this day. I had come too far in dying to self to allow the enemy to hold me to what never belonged to me in the first place. I was living again, whole, healed, and free like never before. Being in the entertainment industry is tough and not a game that can be played and won unless you have Jesus in your heart. I've been through the fire, more in certain parts of the Gospel field than in the secular, to the point where I looked up and realized that everyone who was saying "God" wasn't fully about God. Many had seemed to be more about themselves, and they intentionally or unintentionally used God to pretty much prostitute my gifts for their self-glorification and self-gain. Of course, people can only do what I allow them to, and it hurts. Being taken advantage of, however, seems to happen often when I realize that my heart is pure, and my greatest desire is to expand God's kingdom and do everything for his glory.

Your gifts are supposed to make room for you. Proverbs 18:16 says that your gifts are not supposed to exhaust you, wound you, or suffocate you. But that's what it feels like when the wrong person gets ahold of your heart for God. When they see your power under his anointing in the gifts he has given you, they may say that something is for God, but they really mean it's for them. Yes, even what Satan means for bad, God can turn it around and use it for your good, but it doesn't make right what others did or do "in God's name!" Through God is how the blessings flow. He will use people to help birth the provision for the vision as he chooses and sees fit for his glory.

Question: Why is it that more people are being hurt by the church and in the church, which is what is supposed to be God's bride than actually being hurt by the world that the enemy has taken reign over (with God's permission only)?

Everyone's excuses are that pastors, Christians, religion, and the people of God are human, too. But that is not an excuse! When we chose to walk this walk, we cancelled out being "normal," let alone able to make *being human* an excuse for hurting, belittling, manipulating, judging, condemning, ostracizing, wounding, or breaking people in the body of Christ—or even people not yet a part of the body of Christ…So *knock it off!*

More than thousands of women, including myself, have been victims to this deadly, deceptive, tormenting, poisonous spirit. When we all said *yes* to this walk with Christ, we immediately died to the ways of this world. We were supposed to, anyway, and were filled with the love from Christ to share with every soul in this world. What that church, that man, that friend, that parent, that boss, that death did to you is not your fault so please stop apologizing for what you didn't do.

I was one who always used to say "I'm sorry" all the time, not realizing I was unknowingly apologizing for the anointing God had placed upon me and the destiny he trusted me to carry out. Then a great friend told me, "Rey, you sound like an abused child. You are always apologizing when you haven't done anything wrong. Love, stop saying you're sorry unless you really did something wrong. In that case, you genuinely apologize. Other than that, you have no reason to be sorry. You are amazing and too amazing to be sorry." It was that special day when my whole world changed. I had to change what was keeping me from being the powerful, authentic, and courageous *me* who God had always called me to be.

Stop and Journal

#DAY13
#ITISNTYOURFAULT

"And we know that all things work together for good to them that love God, to them who are the called according to His purpose."
(Romans 8:28 KJV)

JOURNAL #20: (Write these down.)

Question for you:

Remember: Be honest!

I was constantly sorry for being myself and trying to adjust to what everyone else wanted me to be. So many parts of the authentic me died, and it took years to get Reyna back, including getting back my true joy. When people would hurt me or let me down, I automatically blamed myself for it not working or not happening. I would spend days trying to figure out what I did wrong. This was tormenting to my mind, spirit, and my joy of living. I'm absolutely gagging right now because this is who I was for twenty-seven years of my life, and now I'm twenty-eight.

Now, back to you, ladies. What spirit are you going to allow to knock you off your rocker, out of your heels, and back to phase one, which you just conquered and came from? You are an overcomer. You have already won in God's eyes and mine, so why forfeit the win, the greatest win of all time? You are you, and there is only one you. It's time to live again. What and/or are you living with that you need to give an eviction notice to? Tell each one by name to get the hell out of your dwelling place—no more, no more!

Stop and Journal

JOURNAL #21: Write the spirits down by name, and be transparent and honest with God and yourself.

1. What spirits have you been giving life to that need to be evicted from your heart, spirit, body and soul?

2. Speak them out loud, with each one you have written, and seal it by saying this:

"Spirit of _____, I'm calling you out by name. You don't belong here anymore. I bind you and rebuke you, in the name of Jesus. I send you back to the pits of Hell where you came from, in the name of Jesus."

"This is the day that the Lord has made and
I will rejoice and be glad in it."
(Psalms 118:24 KJV)

Now, rest in His presence!

It's your *joy* that keeps you; it's your *joy* that sustains you. It's your *joy* that never fails you. It's your *joy* that brings you forth in victory for his glory. It's in you, and his *joy* rightfully belongs to you. So keep it, use it, and spread it across the nation and world, no matter what. So again, another victory won and another soul can be won on this day. In Jesus's name, amen!

Now rest in his presence!

DAY 14

Nothing Left to Give

Now may the God of peace make you holy in every way,
and may your whole spirit and soul and body be kept
blameless until our Lord Jesus Christ comes again. God will
make this happen, for he who calls you is faithful.

—1 Thessalonians 5:23–24

On day 14, you may be thinking why is this day titled *"Nothing Left to Give?"* It's not your usual: *I'm burnt out, tired, weary in well doing, over it, bewildered, lethargic…* nope! It's all about: *I have nothing else from my past to give life to because I've died to it all. I am leaving it all behind and now giving the whole, healed, and freed me to God, to do all he has called me to do and be.* William McDowell says it perfectly: "I give myself away, I give myself away so you can use me…My life is not my own. To you I belong, I give myself; I give myself to you, Lord."

Begin to be more than okay with the fact that you don't have to identify with the past anymore. "Therefore if any man be in Christ, he is a new creature: old things are passed away; behold, all things are become new" (2 Corinthians 5:17, KJV). You have truly died in order to begin the path and season of living like never before. God loves you, and that's the truth. It may be tough to believe and see through the process, but through these past thirteen days, you trusted him to lead you into the place of being free to just be. No apologizing for being an amazing *you* anymore. Begin to smile and say, "The best is yet to come…It is done. It is well, and it is finished in Jesus's name, amen!"

Stop and Journal

#DAY14
#NOTHINGLEFTTOGIVE

"Now may the God of peace make you holy in every way, and may your whole spirit and soul and body be kept blameless until our Lord Jesus Christ comes again. God will make this happen, for he who calls you is faithful."
(1 Thessalonians 5:23-24)

JOURNAL #22:

Write down your affirmations (words that keep you breathing and living in joy, peace, love, faith, and hope):

These are the affirmations that you will never allow yourself to lose sight of or let go of, even on the good and the tough days that are to come. Rest in this before moving into Day Fifteen: The final day of the process!

You are cherished by all of heaven and a threat to all of hell, but heaven always wins. You getting to the end of day fourteen and stepping into day fifteen is proof in itself that heaven has truly won once again. Rest in this before moving into day fifteen: The final day of the process!

> I will sing of the mercies of the Lord for ever: with my mouth will I make known thy faithfulness to all generations. For I have said, mercy shall be built up for ever: thy faithfulness shalt thou establish in the very heavens. (Psalms 89: 1–2, KJV)

DAY 15

The Revelation

Let all the inhabitants of the world stand in awe of Him. For
He spake and it was done; he commanded, and it stood fast.

—Psalms 33:8–9 (KJV)

On day 15, you may be asking yourself: "Is this real?" Here is your answer from the Lord that he shared with me for you to have peace and know that it is well: He expressed that this is real! For we, as his daughters, have gone through each day, holding his hand and experiencing his forever sufficient grace and unfailing love. Beloved, this is one of the realest moments we will ever remember and experience as we continue to take his ordained steps into destiny. He has called you, destined you, chosen you, appointed you, and approved you for such a time as this. You picking up this book and reading it this far is the ultimate proof, and he is a God who shall never lie. All that he has promised you; all the dreams that were embedded in you from when you were just a child come solely from him.

He placed those thoughts, those visions, those joys, and triumphs there in the depths of your heart, spirit, and soul. So in that, know that from this day forth, it shall be done, and it will all come to pass. He is absolutely in love with you, his child, and adores everything about you. He made you blemish free, whole, and healed, only to live free. The price has already been paid. For he knows all, sees all, and does all within a wink of an eye.

All that you went through, he was there! All that you have seen, he was there! All that you stood up to, he was there! All that broke you down, only to build you up, he was there! All that caused pain and heartache, he was there! All that birthed triumph and victory, he was there! Every tear that was shed, he was there to wash away and redeem! He was there; he is here, and he is not ever leaving you! You are his, and he is yours, for he used all of this to create in you what he needed and destined you to be simply because you were and are worth it. What is gold if it is not refined through the fire? Impure and worth way less than it should be if it was not taken through the fire.

You made it, beloved. By faith, you made it, his beloved!

Read Hebrews 11, which perfectly defines faith.

What is there he won't and/or cannot do for you? He speaks and things have to fall in alignment. If he calls every star out by name, every single night, and knows every single hair on your head, what can he not do for you? Trust him and have faith in him. Just as you showed up and trusted this process on your 30-day journey, you know that he honors obedience and faith, even when it's not much bigger than the size of a mustard seed. It is your time. There's no need to look back because the future is so clear now. You have died in order to really begin to live in who he has always intended for you to become…to be in destiny with him. Get ready, his queen, for you have arrived at the best point of your entire life, and he is promising you that your life will never be the same, in the name of his son, Jesus Christ, amen!

You have been made whole, healed, and free! Now, let's do destiny as the *complete* you.

Stop and Journal

#DAY15
#THEREVELATION

"…let all the inhabitants of the world stand in awe of Him. For
He spake and it was done; he commanded, and it stood fast."
(Psalms 33:8-9 KJV)

You have been made whole, healed, and free!
Now, let's do destiny as you complete your journey!

JOURNAL #23: Write a true testament of faith to the new you:

PART 2

The Breakthrough

Remember ye not the former things, neither consider the things of old. Behold, I will do a new thing; now it shall spring forth; shall ye not know it? I will even make a way in the wilderness, and rivers in the desert.

—Isaiah 43:18–19 (KJV)

DAY 16

Believing Again

Faith Defined

Now faith is the substance of things hoped for, evidence of things not seen. For by it the elders obtained a good report. Through faith we understand that the words were framed by the word of God, so that things which are seen were not made of things which do appear. by faith Abel offered unto God a more excellent sacrifice than Cain, by which He obtained witness that he was righteous, God testifying of his gifts; and by it he being dead yet speaketh. By faith Enoch was translated that he should not see death; and was not found, because God had translated him: for before that his translation he had this testimony, that he pleased God. But without faith it is impossible to please him: for he that cometh to God must believe that he is, and that he is a rewarder of them that diligently seek him. By faith Noah, being warned of God of things not seen as yet, moved with fear, prepared heir of the righteousness which is by faith. By faith Abraham, when he was called to go out into a place which he should after receive for an inheritance, obeyed; and he went out, not knowing whither he went. By faith He sojourned in the land of promise, as in a strange country, dwelling in tabernacles with Isaac and Jacob, The heirs with him of the same promise. For he looked for a city which hath foundations, whose builder and maker is God. Through faith Also Sara herself received strength to conceive seed, and was delivered of a child when she was past age, because she judged him faithful who had promised. *(Hebrews 11:1–11, KJV)*

Stop and Journal

#DAY16
#BELIEVINGAGAIN

Hebrews 11:1-11 KJV
(Write down what this passage did to your spirit, mind, and heart when you read it.)

Now, take a listen to:

"Ressurecting"
by Elevation Worship
(You can access it on iTunes.)

Take in all that this beautiful song is saying, and allow God to soothe your soul!

"To appoint unto them that mourn in Zion, to give unto them beauty for ashes, the oil of joy for mourning, the garment of praise for the spirit of heaviness; that they might be called trees of righteousness, the planting of the LORD, that he might be glorified."
(Isaiah 61:3 KJV)

On day 16, you must take a moment to take a deep breath. As you do that, take another moment to realize that you survived, and you were always *destined to survive*!

I know not everyone reading this book is saved, but I prayed for it to be that way. If you have a relationship with Jesus or not, he loves you, and he wanted me to develop this blueprint to prove that to you. His love is real, and it's never leaving your side. He already paid the ultimate price for you; the day he died on the cross. On that third day, he rose again so we could live and have eternal life. After all that I had to overcome, this was all I needed in order to believe again. My heart would always take me to this familiar place; this is the place that has kept me through every season.

In expressing God's love for you, I want to take this moment to say thank you to you amazing women in breakthrough. Thank you for having an open heart and allowing me to share my journey with you as you begin to complete yours, too. Can I be honest? None of this has been easy for me, in any way, and at some points, I have played it safe.

Due to the position I'm in in the entertainment industry (faith-based and secular) and within my family, I felt like I had to play it safe because I didn't want to be judged. It took an amazing man of God and friend, Marc Cunningham (director/actor/writer), to tell me, "Rey, what is this journey if you don't tell the fullness of your story, the mistakes, the falls, the bruises, and the broken relationships? Explain to the women why you are *still* fighting to believe. Tell them and don't hold back so that God can deliver them the exact same way he is about to deliver you. Your breakthrough is in your testimony being shared, and their breakthrough is through you sharing your story."

How many of you ladies know that as soon as you step into a good place, mentally, emotionally, physically, and spiritually, there are certain things that transpire to wiggle you into remembering parts of your past? The areas that you still haven't quite dealt with; the parts of your past that you have been staying away from and no longer praying about. Yep, that was a specific part of the shift in my life as I stepped into *breakthrough* and *believing again*. That was the weekend I began to write this chapter of the book.

During that time, my ex, who God had told me to release three months prior, came to California for his TV show's promo events. In the midst of receiving his text informing me that he was in town, my niece was born. The next day, my best friend, Michelle, walked down the aisle on her wedding day.

These events took place in twenty-four hours, and everything shifted for me. While all three of these pivotal events were happening, I recognized what the enemy was trying to keep me from. God was showing me what he has for me if I let go of my past, completely in obedience to his instructions spoken to me three months before. The proof in this was when I went from being an authentic Reyna—goofy, fun, random, and had everyone falling on the floor, laughing all day—to the old Reyna who was supposedly dead from day one through day fifteen. It was a joy to see my ex, but the new me was tucked away, and the old serious unsure me re-surfaced again. And until this very day, I was still living as a victim to one last thing concerning my past. By faith, I am able to open up to you about the greatest struggle of my life.

My story was supposed to be "I'm saving myself for marriage." My heart's greatest desire was to stay a virgin until my "Prince Charming" swept me off my feet and married me. I was the one daughter left to do things perfectly. That was supposed to be how things would happen. And it was until every relationship I had stepped into painted me as the "main, number one girl/woman" to the kind of men who always had other women; the type of women who could fulfill their needs while they were with the "virgin/trophy" me.

This caused me a lot of brokenness and a lot of pain. I went from being the most confident woman in every atmosphere I stepped into, to beginning to feel like I was never enough. It left many scars, and I hated the fact that every time I got into a relationship, I was ending it not too long after. This was because of the man's unfaithfulness and/or lack of honor and respect for me, my destiny, and my pure heart. I was that trophy they carried on their arm to make their parents, teammates, managers, agents, and preachers proud. With me being pure, they then would put me away on the shelf, and in that moment, I wasn't enough for them to stay out of another woman's bedroom. I felt like I was failing, and the enemy had me thinking something was wrong with me that I needed to change something in order to keep a man committed and faithful to me.

I kept apologizing to God and asking him to change me and make me a better woman. Wow. Yes, I just said it. I begin to *apologize* for who I was and asked God to fix me and make me a better woman so I could keep a man faithful to me. Mind you, most guys I had dated were men of God. Now, looking back, I realize they were men of God who just hadn't grown up and become kings yet.

What this pattern did to me and my destiny—along with my self-worth and confidence—was terrifying! It took me from who I was always meant to be in God and in destiny, unashamed of my anointing, to lowering myself and forgetting why I was keeping myself pure in the first place—which was for God and me. It wrecked my "kingdom authority" in spirit and in truth and tainted my anointing as I began to question my calling. I ended up giving myself away to a man I was dating, thinking that this one I could finally keep faithful to me. I thought it would break the cycle I had been living, and that it would change everything. But I was wrong!

I didn't want anything to do with God because I was angry. I was angry with myself, and with the fact that he would even allow the enemy to oppress me to the point of me being okay with giving away the greatest part of me: my innocence and my purity. The one thing I had left with which to show my gratitude toward God. Even through years of celibacy and minor slip-ups, it took me five years to truly forgive myself for this. The guilt and condemnation the enemy consistently used had me wrapped around his finger. I was constantly thinking in one breath that I was worthless, and in the other that I had the power now—that it was the only way—to get and keep a man.

Do you see how Satan works? My confidence in God was non-existent, and my confidence in my appearance and sex appeal had taken the lead. I didn't make a lifestyle of being intimate with every boyfriend or guy I dated. But it was the idea that I could have whatever man I wanted because I allowed the spirits to transfer onto me, leading a lustful lifestyle from being tapped into my sexuality. I didn't have to do anything; it showed through my paid appearances as a name in the industry. In the way I dressed; the way I walked into a room; the drinks I had, and the way I looked at a man.

Something in me died, and something not of me began to live. Every day I woke, I was crying, asking God to give me back myself. I felt so empty and knew I was living out a different story that didn't belong to me. I never felt worthy of any blessing or any booking. It was hard to preach a sermon to young girls and even harder to visit my family, along with getting on my knees to pray daily. I understood more than ever why God's Word says to keep yourself pure and untouched until you're married. Not only are the soul ties deadly, but it's a dangerous place to be once you tap into that realm and allow Satan to have his way with you. Take a look at 1 Corinthians 7:1–40 and 1 Thessalonians 4:1–18 (ESV) for further study. I made a lot of bad decisions all because I opened that one huge door. But God's grace in that built, in the depths of my soul, a testimony out of this world. This is how this book was really conceived. *I never felt like I was enough* after this downfall, when not feeling like I was enough was why I fell down this path in the first place. Do you see the cycle?

With God, in God, and through God, I was always more than enough, but men who weren't whole became my reflection because I was dating the opposite of who I was, what I was, and what I stood for in Christ.

> And have no fellowship with the unfruitful works of darkness, but rather reprove them. (Ephesians 5:11, KJV)

God had to clean up so much damage I had done and had to show me his truth in it all. He showed me who I made a boyfriend, when they were actually my assignment to help lead and draw closer to the hem of his garment. He showed me who was never supposed to be able to get close to me, but my fear of being alone allowed them into my God-Destined story. He showed me where he gave me every sign to run, saying, "Don't go there!" to the moments where I had stopped, looked up to Heaven, and continued to grab the hand of a man instead of the hand of my Heavenly father. He loved me in spite of my constant mess-ups. He cleaned me up and held me every time I cried myself through the pain of living a life that didn't belong to me. He began to give me beauty for my ashes:

> To appoint unto them that mourn in Zion, to give unto them beauty for ashes, the oil of joy for mourning, the garment of praise for the spirit of heaviness; that they might be called trees of righteousness, the planting of the Lord, that he might be glorified. (Isaiah 61:3, KJV)

God loved the hell out of me and loved the heaven back into my bloodstream. I was dying, and he restored me. But in that restoration period, I couldn't get out of my head what someone had once told me: "Because you lost your virginity, you will never have the man that God has for you now." It felt like someone had taken my insides and twisted them up until I had no more breath left to take in. It pierced me so deep to the point where it took me a little over five years to become free from the bondage that sentenced placed upon me. It was on Friday, August 8, 2014 when I finally became free. The number eight equals "new beginnings." (Biblestudy.org, The Meaning of Number 8)

I write this, telling you that up until this chapter and this very day, I still doubted God would bring my "king" because I had been so used and used to attracting the ones who didn't quite understand my anointing from God—or what it meant to be a king to a queen. They didn't know God's love enough to allow him to make them whole, healed, and free. They weren't able to seek me properly, due to a lack of seeking God first to learn how to love, cherish, honor, and find me in destiny.

The one won't do what the others have done. He will be what the others could never be because they weren't meant to be my forever in destiny!

Now this is true breakthrough, and in this very moment, I am beginning to believe in the promises of God concerning my king again. Believing in God's promises doesn't cost you a thing. But not believing could possibly cost you everything because it is all by faith, in faith, and with faith that God manifests on Earth what's already been done in Heaven on your behalf!

Stop and Journal

JOURNAL #24: (Write your truth)

1. What is it that I need to finally be free from?

2. What does "breakthrough" mean to me?

3. How do I break free from this thing?

4. When did I stop believing?

5. What do I need to do in order to believe again?

Me…you…we are so worth it! Believe again!

I praise God for each of you women. Because of you, I can look in the mirror and begin to see what and who God sees in me, and what worth I carry in just being a daughter of the King. I…you… *we* are so *worth it!*

We are being and have been set free to be!

DAY 17

Fearless

Fearless: Lacking fear, bold, brave, courageous, intrepid, valiant, valorous, gallant, plucky, lionhearted, heroic, daring, audacious, indomitable, doughty (Google.com definition of Fearless)

On day 17, I know I speak for us all when I say we are standing on solid fertile holy ground. Something about "believing again" resonated within my spirit so profoundly from day sixteen, that I felt *free to just be* on this day. How do *you* feel? Be completely honest with yourself; because as you should remember, it's the only way that this journey and "the process to the breakthrough" works effectively and efficiently.

I can tell you from the depths of my being that I feel like I can finally breathe. Something happened to me, for me, and with me, all because of yesterday's #TransparencyMoment. I became fearless in that very moment when I let it all go. The things that are considered our greatest struggle are the things we keep hidden and tucked away, as if they don't exist. By doing so, we give them power to keep living and to keep consuming our presence as a whole. How will we ever *become* if we don't overcome the fear of people's judgment or of people knowing what keeps us up at night, crying for freedom to just be able to *be*? The only way to overcome fear is by flushing it out with faith.

Stop and Journal

#DAY17
#FEARLESS

Fearless: lacking fear
Synonyms: bold, brave, courageous, intrepid,
valiant, valorous, gallant, plucky, lionhearted, heroic,
daring, audacious, indomitable, doughty
(Google definition of "fearless")

JOURNAL #25: Write your own definition of "faith:"

So, what has fear been keeping you from?

Whatever that thing is,
"Just do it."

What does it hurt to believe that you can actually live *free* from everything that once had you held in bondage, suffocating? Fear keeps you from what you don't need to be kept from and has you running to what God never intended for you to go to and through. On this day, I want to help each of you to become so fearless that nothing, and I mean *nothing*, can take you off course ever again—at least in a way—that you allowed certain things to before.

Every day, there is something; every day, there is another obstacle to face and something to overcome, but that's just it: *to overcome*...not to affirm yourself in anything that is outside of what God says concerning you. Any time something comes toward you that's able to take away your peace and joy, you immediately know it's not of God, and you rebuke it in Jesus's name and speak the opposite of what that thing is trying to press upon you. In that moment is when you have again become fearless and faith-filled instead of fearful. It's a mindset, and in faith alone, the definition (refer to your journal) states that having faith means you have complete trust or confidence in someone or something.

So just as you have faith, trust, and confidence in God and believe in him, you must absolutely have faith in yourself, trust in yourself, have confidence in yourself, and believe in yourself the way

God has always called you to! How else can you step into destiny and fearlessly become the best you? There is no other way. The thing is, there aren't any shortcuts this time. Step in and don't waver; because if you have that vision and dream burning in the depths of your soul, and it keeps you up at night, that means God placed it in you and claimed it for you and only you to do. That's being *fearless*. Taking the passion and running with it, causing it to press you forward, and believing in the process in order to begin to live that thing out every single day.

So what has *fear* been keeping you from?

This is a question you must ask yourself so you know and can identify what you need to become fearless, too. The process has been completed, but it's in the breakthrough that the overflow of understanding and security comes in the identity of knowing who and whose you are, without question or doubt. *Fearless* says that when everyone and everything is telling me *no*, I *go* and do exactly what God has told me *yes* to.

Distinctively knowing God's voice within your spirit is extremely important at all times so you can begin to believe outside of what people have labeled you as. Even with the new you, there will be new labels and new obstacles, but it's how you handle them and what you do with them that shows how far you've come from where you were, to where you are about to go. It shows the world and those who aren't for your success how much of a threat you are to the enemy and his set-ups, which now become your ultimate "bless-ups."

This is the problem that we had to leave in the first half of this journey. You have to continue to leave behind the people who you let in and allowed to be a part of your daily life weren't technically called to be a part of your destined life story. If they weren't written, developed, created, and approved to be a part of your life story by God himself, they must go. During the breakthrough, you must let the labelers go! You are who God says you are, and being *fearless* is a huge part of that definition. So…*just do it.*

Let them go, too, because what it may cost you to keep them could be everything that you've fought so hard to be free from. There are too many lives attached to your purpose. Are your labelers/friends worth all of those lives lost? I'm only saying what God had brought to me during this time of my journey. God and you have to matter so much more because at that very moment is when you literally begin to change the world. Let them go! That's being *fearlessly whole*...seeing yourself without the baggage and in hands' reach of your entire destiny as it unfolds in the presence of your enemies.

Yes, choose love, choose to forgive, and most importantly, choose to let go so you can fly. That was a part of you when you were broken and bruised, and it can't be a part of you when you are restored and healed. We've all tried it, and it simply just doesn't work. You will always be reminded of who you were and not who you've become from proving people wrong and letting it all go.

> Fearless says,
> I can stand alone and feel complete!
> Fearless says,
> I am me, and there's no other amazing way to be!
> Fearless says,
> I will believe in all that God has promised me.
> Fearless says,
> I will no longer answer to my emotions but my integrity.
> Fearless says,
> I am equipped for this and ready for all that is to come.
> Fearless says,
> I will go where God says go, stop when he says stop, and be where he needs me to be, continually and consistently.
> Fearless says,
> I won't look back because I am not my past; I'm whole, healed, and free.
> Fearless says,
> I am fearfully and wonderfully made. (Psalms 139:14, KJV)
> Fearless says, I am...

Something stopped me as I was writing these *fearless* verses down...I'm still having a hard time believing that *I am more than enough* for all that God has awaiting me. I continually ask God: how do I get out of this place and space? This way of thinking is a curse to my destiny and calling. If I'm saying that I am not enough, then I'm ultimately saying that God is not enough, even though he created me and made me perfectly in the likeness of his image. It sucks that many of us as women can't seem to grasp the fact that *we are amazing and more than enough.* What is the breakthrough without this understanding and this way of living day in and out?

So check this: I was quiet long enough to hear God's voice say, "It doesn't happen overnight, baby!" My God, this word and revelation pierced me in my side because that's the part of us left that we must be free from. Nobody can tell you or make you believe that you are more than enough. Only we, ourselves, can. Each day we wake, we have to fearlessly make it a point to say to ourselves: no matter where I've been, no matter what I've done or didn't do, no matter how much time I feel I've lost…how much weight I've gained…how many men I've been with… "I am more than enough, and I am fearfully and wonderfully made to live fearlessly in destiny!"

Stop and Journal

JOURNAL #26: Write eight of your own "Fearless says" declarations. Speak them over yourself each and every single day! Place them on individual post-it notes, if needed, on your mirror.

Fearless says…

Fearless says…

Fearless says…

Fearless says…

Fearless says…

Fearless says…

Fearless says…

Fearless says…

Let's get into the true essence of unfailing faith. Are you ready?

DAY 18

Unfailing Faith

*Jesus saith unto her, "Said I not unto thee, that, if thou
wouldest believe, thou shouldest see the glory of God?"*

—John 11:40 (KJV)

On the day 18, it's quite simple; your faith will change your whole atmosphere and your day-to-day way of living. So what do you think believing will cost you? When you step into the breakthrough of believing, you step into the true essence of becoming all God has called you, destined you, appointed you, approved you, and anointed you to be! Everything starts and ends with faith.

Just as we read before, it was all by faith that what once wasn't, became what is now, and without faith, it possibly could've never come to fruition. This means that you believing isn't just for you. It's also for all of Heaven, which is continually backing you up, in order for God to begin a new thing here on Earth—through you, with you, for you, and for this entire world. You have something on the inside of you that only faith can pull out and bring forth. You are more than enough, but you're not big enough to do it on your own...

It requires God, faith in him and faith in yourself. But it's crazy faith that, no matter what you see around you, you stand on the facts of God's promises, and it will come to pass. God doesn't care what's in your bank account, on your call log, on your voicemail, the number of your credit score, the bills left to pay, the repossession of your car, the lack of finding a church home, your children doing everything but his will…it *doesn't matter*. He will see you through because it's through your faith that he is moved. His hand is in acceleration mode. By faith! He is not moved by circumstances or life-altering situations. Why? Because he is God! He is God, all by himself.

One thing that God had to check me on, in a loving way, was that he is not human, and he is not affected or infected by the way we do things, in any way, shape, or form. That's when the breakthrough in believing begins to manifest when you start to see God for who he really and truly is, instead of what your emotions or mind have tried to define him as. He is indescribable and uncontainable. He can't be limited in any way, and because we are of him, we can't be limited either; it's only by our lack of faith in him, concerning our lives, that places limits on what we can do. He can do whatever he chooses when he chooses to do it, but sometimes, he withholds certain things because we are not being ready to receive it.

Sometimes, being ready is just waking up every day, living as if it has already happened, standing in the truth of your promise and not compromising anything concerning the chosen *you*. When you live in such a way, God then says, "She is ready. I can present it to her now." It's a faith that exceeds what the human eye can see and even think. It's where you die to doubt, fear, shame, condemnation, ridicule, and self-sabotaging moments and you say, "If God said it, it is so! If he put it in me, it shall be done! If he has been keeping me, it is yet still to come! Until then, I will stay in my secret place and be ready for my promise from God and God alone!" Having unwavering faith is a choice that must continually be made each and every single day we wake.

Stop and Journal

#DAY18
#UNFAILINGFAITH

The Power of Faith
"Jesus saith unto her, 'Said I not unto thee, that, if thou wouldest believe, thou shouldest see the glory of God?'"
(John 11:40 KJV)

You are more than enough, but you're not
big enough to do it on your own…

If God said it, it is so! If He put it in me, it shall be done! If He has been keeping me, it is yet still to come! Until then, I will stay in my secret place and be ready for my promise from God and God alone!

JOURNAL #27: Write the breakdown of Hebrews 11:1 that is described in the book:

If you look at today, today was once unseen, yet yesterday, you were talking about today as if it was already here. You had your calendars set; your appointments notated, and your outfit picked out. Ready and prepped for your day, yes you were. That is faith!

You didn't know that today would come, but you lived as though it was already here, knowing that you would wake up today and do exactly what had been set out for you to do. You even put your bookmark in this book to prepare for where you would start reading next, still not knowing if today would come. Just in faith, you positioned yourself to become a *greater you* for the next day God would bring. That is faith! So what are you waiting for in order to start believing beyond what you see? You have already been doing this on a daily basis.

God's plan for our lives is unraveling before us. At times, in destiny, there seems to be a blockage that causes us to completely hold back. Then in due season, at God's perfect timing, the blockage begins to effortlessly open up right before us. All that we have desired and worked so hard for, God freely presents to us as a gift from the heavens above. In this, we feel his presence and the power of his glory as we see how he operates with ease in this world. Our weaknesses are not to be feared; they simply allow the power and glory of God to perform most brilliantly.

As we press forth and triumph along the path God has chosen for us, solely depending on his strength to keep us, we must expect to see miracles. The miracles that he presents are not always visible to the naked eye, but we can see them clearly, as we live by faith and not by sight. This is what enables us to see his glory.

Reference scriptures: take a moment to read these scriptures below…

Psalms 63:2
2 Corinthians 5:7
John 11:40

It's Your Time

Begin to be the first one to believe in yourself and no longer the last. Start to encourage yourself day in and day out, as you live out what you are now choosing to believe. It's in you, and I believe that on this day, you will be a walking testament of what happens even when you have faith no larger than the size of a mustard seed. The process is complete; it's time for your *full breakthrough*. Every area of your life is about to be shaken beyond your control because your faith is going to stir up a major move of God, here on Earth. Go where you've never gone; do what you've never done; say what he tells you to say, and stand for all he has called you to stand for.

In this, you will become all that you never even knew you could be, in him, for his glory, fully stepping into destiny. Give him your *yes* in faith and show him, with your actions, that you believe so that your walk matches your talk. Stay in it. You are right there, beloved. *Right there*. It may not ever make sense, but when it's God speaking to your spirit, it will one day make all of the sense in the world. I promise you; someone's life will depend on it.

Stop and Journal

Take a read and reference these scriptures:
Psalm 63:2
2 Corinthians 5:7
John 11:40

JOURNAL #28:

1. Write down your dreams (What burns passionately deep inside?):

2. Write down what He has spoken to your spirit:

3. Write down the things that require the most faith:

4. Write at the end: It is done, it is well, and it is finished in Jesus' name, amen!

DAY 19

What It Really Means to Be Okay and Even Better

*Not that I speak from want, for I have learned to be content
in whatever circumstances I am. I know how to get along with
humble means, and I also know how to live in prosperity; in
any and every circumstance I have learned the secret of being
filled and going hungry, both of having abundance and suffering
need. I can do all things through Him who strengthens me.*

—Philippians 4:11–13 (NKJV)

On the day 19, you step into the place of understanding that
it is well with you. You have experienced the beginning of
the breakthrough in *believing again* and being *fearless* in
your *unfailing faith*.

Have the first three days been easy thus far?

Definitely not, but just as mentioned before, it's a choice to see
yourself past the *old you* as you have been pressing into becoming
the *new you*. Today, you have to come to a place of realizing that in
all the days of your life, when you weren't quite okay and everything
felt as if it was continually falling apart, it was for such a day as this.
It's when you can look in the mirror and continue to say, "Beloved, I
have survived, and my best days are in this moment right now." This
is when you choose to be okay beyond any backlash, attack, doubt,
question, judgment, or inside voice that is telling you anything other
than "you can do this."

Being okay and even better is saying that in the midst of it all, I choose to no longer allow anything to take me off course from what I know and have come into agreement with for my life, from God alone. It's the day that you wake up, take in the fact that you are *becoming*, and that you are amazing for even accepting this God-Ordained journey. A lot of times, we are so used to going through a stress-filled routine, that when we aren't going through anything, we feel compelled to create that stress-filled atmosphere in what actually is a peaceful and God-Sustaining place. One thing I had to learn was that life doesn't have to be hard, painful, stressful, fearful, overbearing, destructive, or even uneasy.

When we have God, life can be light, peaceful, gentle, nurturing, cultivating, breathtaking, and full of his glory. I learned that it's a choice to live in the weight of life or in the light of life. I was one who only knew how to live in the weight of it all and couldn't enjoy the moments when I was in the light of it. Living this way took away my joy of living in destiny and in being a woman, authentically.

Part of the breakthrough is acknowledging what life you have been leading and what life you should instead be leading and desire to lead. By this day, you are already in it. You are in the light of life. Please, I ask you not to go back to the weight. Never forget that God says, *"Come unto me, all ye that labour and are heavy laden, and I will give you rest. Take my yoke upon you, and learn of me; for I am meek and lowly in heart: and ye shall find rest unto your souls. For my yoke is easy, and my burden is light" (Matthew 11: 28–30, KJV).*

Ultimately, what I am trying to express is that you deserve so much more than what you might think. And that much more comes when we begin to no longer live in the place of lack but in the place of expectancy. We have to expect God to be God and to keep his promises beyond what we can understand. The abundance comes when we place our thoughts in his hands and receive his thoughts concerning us in all things. He is a God who does not lie, and in that alone, we must know that choosing to be okay and better is an outward, daily expression to God, saying that we are ready for the increase he has awaiting us. It's the mindset that we choose to take in our daily lives that can instantly change our present situation.

No more lack.
No more expecting heartbreak.
No more emotional rollercoasters.
No more discouragement.
No more settling.
No more expecting less than God's best.
No more being anything other than the authentic you.
No more second-guessing.
No more standing in a poverty mindset.
No more complacency.
No more,
Because you are worth so much more!

Stop and Journal

#DAY19
#WHATITREALLYMEANSTOBEOKAY
#ANDEVENBETTER

"Not that I speak from want, for I have learned to be
content in whatever circumstances I am. I know how
to get along with humble means, and I also know how
to live in prosperity; in any and every circumstance I
have learned the secret of being filled and going hungry,
both of having abundance and suffering need. I can
do all things through Him who strengthens me…"
(Philippians 4:11-13)

JOURNAL #29: Write down your "no mores":

1. Be very specific and detailed on what you are saying "no more" to:

2. What will you no longer identify yourself with?

3. What will you speak over yourself to step into the new?

Dear God,
    Here is what I'm afraid of _____
_____ (Fill in your fear here.)

It's okay to be okay and even better!
Choose to be okay.
Choose to be better.
Choose to be you, authentically!

Begin to believe so much, that what was always destined for you begins to be naturally drawn to you. Be fearless in knowing that you didn't have to do anything to earn God's love; there's nothing you have to do in order to keep it, and there's nothing you could possibly do to lose it. Through faith, you know this and realize that this is a part of his promise. The same way he has love for you is the same way he does destiny with and through you. You didn't earn your destiny. He is not looking for you to be perfect in order for you to live it out, and it's up to you to just say yes to it.

More than anything, what he is saying is, "I trust you!" He wouldn't have placed such a calling and such profound gifts within you if he didn't know that you could execute them. With the three steps (mentioned in your journal) beginning to form a solid foundation in your daily life, it will be so much easier to know that it's okay to be okay and better without feeling guilty for being able to say, "I am full of joy, and I am actually okay today!"

I was at Robi Reed (BET casting Director) and Dr. Holly Carter's (Executive Producer of Preachers of LA) "Ascend" Bible study recently, and my brother, Devon Franklin, was preaching. He started off his message with having us take out our cell phones to write in our notes app so we would not lose that moment in time of truth. He told each of us to write:

Dear God, here's what I'm afraid of… (Reference this in your journal and follow the instructions.) For the first time in my entire life, I couldn't write anything at all. It was that very evening that I realized there was nothing I was afraid of anymore. All fear had been wiped away, and for the first time, I realized I was finally living.

So as the message went on, I began to try to think of things that I was possibly still fearful of. In my mind, I began to create things that were no longer a part of my story of who I had stepped in to and become in Christ. In reality, I wasn't afraid of anything. And in that moment, I became fearful of not having fear dwelling with in me anymore. God stopped me right there and said, "It is finished. You are *the you* who I always intended you to be; don't go back there, and don't do that to yourself again. Stay in this place of knowing me and knowing that I am doing a new thing that fear can no longer coexist with!"

It's okay to be okay and even better!

Choose to be okay.

Choose to be better.

Choose to be you, *authentically*!

DAY 20

One Day at a Time

Take therefore no thought for the marrow:
for the morrow shall take thought for the things of itself.
Sufficient unto the day is the evil thereof.

—Matthew 6:34 (KJV)

Day 20 is about understanding that patience is the greatest gift you can give yourself during this day-to-day process of becoming whole, healed, and free to step into destiny. Even in choosing to be okay over being affected by the things that used to pierce your side needs patience and grace. Live in today, remembering what you learned about yourself yesterday and not worrying about the next day. You've been given today; make the best of it and decide on what you need to do for you, this new you; the you who you may need to start getting to know from scratch.

Beloved, you are God's joy, and he is so in awe of you. You've come so far; too far to turn back now. So give yourself the time you need to take it all in and understand that you are now being equipped to step into that thing, or those things that you gave up on, or let go of, due to the tragedies. Instead, remind yourself that *the process* of this 30-day journey has completely washed away all of that. You have a clean slate now, and your definition of who you were to yourself should have completely changed. You overcame it all, beloved, and one day at a time, you must now choose to step out, step up, and step into the greatness that rightfully belongs to you.

God once spoke to me and said, "My daughter, all I need is for you to do is show up, and I will show out. You are my joy, and nothing can change that, but I need you to allow me to be God. You are not built to birth these visions on your own. One day at a time, if you can surrender to me, I can do what I've been desiring to do with you, in you, through you, and for you, along with this world. I love you. I don't quite think you fully understand that just yet, my beloved. So in that, let's work on you. I hear your heart, and I see what you are facing, but it's not too big for me, and it will never outshine my glory."

Then I spoke to God in transparency, saying this: "Lord, I don't know how to just be. Still at this part of the journey, I can't quite grasp the fact that everything is just the way it's supposed to be. The one thing, Lord, I can't quite have peace with and understand is why I can't be okay with not being married yet. Sometimes I cry, day in and day out, thanking you for my future husband but wondering deep down where he is and why he hasn't found me yet."

"I know I've made some mistakes, and I know that I've showed you I wasn't ready. But when you allow one who meets every desire of my heart to come into my life, I begin to get my hopes up and assume he is my king. When he begins to bring much healing, joy, and restoration to my faith in your truth, God, his consistency then changes drastically. And mine stays the same. I become confused, along with feeling rejected. Lord, you know who I'm talking about without me having to say a word. My heart is heavy because this immediately takes me back to that place of feeling like I did something wrong, or that I'm not enough!"

"I refuse to go back to this place, Lord...I need you to sustain me in this season. God, I just need you; I want you, and I want to know that everything will come to pass because of you. Help me love myself the way you love me. Help me be patient and breathe as I take this pain, truth, and his deception one day at a time! Lord, I trust you with me. I trust you with my destiny, career, and calling. I trust you for my friends and family, but this one area left that I can't quite surrender to you is concerning my future king. I need your help, Lord. My tears are from feeling like I failed again because of the shift in this relationship that I thought deep down had obviously come from you. I was wrong."

After I laid it all out at his throne, I made my way over to my Ms. Lori Roberts, and tears fell from my eyes without any more fighting on the inside of me, as soon as I arrived. God spoke to my spirit, saying, "It feels like history is repeating itself, but who says it's repeating anything? Let it be! Trust the process and be patient."

As my dearest friend gave me the nickname, "Big, big revelation," and that is exactly what that moment with God was: a big, big revelation. I could have chosen for it to be a repeat of my past and allow it to take me there. Instead, I chose to be better, greater, wiser, stronger, and to love myself more than ever. In that moment, Ms. Lo and I began to giggle because deep within, I (again) already had the solution to my problem. Immediately, I died to that huge part of my past and stepped even further into just being the greater, God-Fulfilled *me*. I chose to not allow it to be history repeating itself again. I chose to hear God's voice and receive his ultimate protection of my heart, mind, body, and spirit so I wouldn't waver in my destiny. And in all of this, I chose to let go of what couldn't accept me for the *true me* who had finally come back to life in the depths and center of myself. I chose to take it one day at a time, and I chose *me*.

Wow, I chose *me*. It was something I had never really done before—and without an apology. This time, an apology wasn't necessary because I was obedient to God in not allowing anything to take me away from myself. This consisted of God's joy that has been embedded in me, to stand with me and for me at all costs, through anything and everything.

Stop and Journal

#DAY20
#ONEDAYATATIME

"Take therefore no thought for the marrow: for the
morrow shall take thought for the things of itself.
Sufficient unto the day is the evil thereof."
(Matthew 6:34 KJV)

JOURNAL #30: Write the truth…

1. What's the one thing that needs a little truth and attention within you?

2. What and/or who do you need to completely give to God?

3. What action needs to be taken in order to progress one day at a time?

4. What does my life look like during this process?

In this moment, stay present in acknowledging what you
need to release and what it takes for you to do exactly
that! Once again, it's because you are worth it!

Taking it all in one day at a time allows you to *just be* as everything unfolds. In your patience and consistency, you will allow yourself to grow from all of this and into all that's needed to build yourself in to the *new you*. It will lay down an unbreakable and unshakable foundation. No matter what may come, you will not be shaken because this time, you've been built back up on solid ground. You must know, more now than ever, that you are worth every second of time that it takes for you to see the masterpiece that God is sculpting with you, from the inside out, for your life, as he tells your true story!

In this, tomorrow has no other choice but to be even greater than today. So take it one day at a time. Why? Because you are worth it!

DAY 21

Beginning to Grow in Love with God

Grow: *to arise or issue as a natural development from*
an original happening, circumstance, or source
Love: *a profoundly tender, passionate affection for another person*
God: *the one Supreme Being, the creator and ruler of the Universe*
(Father, Son, and Holy Spirit) (Google: dictionary.reference.com)

On day 21, you must realize that, after all you have experienced in life and pressed through, you didn't do it by yourself. Not one moment of it was done alone. In knowing that, there naturally was a symbolic growth that began, and one that can't go unacknowledged. You began to grow in love with God.

The who, what, when, where, how, and why may be a few of the questions you have concerning how this began to take place while on this journey. Think about it for a second and realize that it wasn't forced—it just happened. The moment you said, "I need to take *The 30-Day Journey to Loving the Woman in Me*," you petitioned all of Heaven to take its rightful place in your life as you began to step into the fullness of your God-Ordained destiny. You perhaps picked up this book because there was a fire burning on the inside of you. You knew you needed to love yourself in a way that you have never before experienced. The only way to truly do that is to understand the love of God and the endless love that he has for you.

This is the revelation of a lifetime. It's here and now: the wonders of God and growing in love with him!

Who:

God is Alpha and Omega, the beginning and the end... Who is, who was, and who is to come; the Almighty. He is the true God; he is the living God and an everlasting king... He has made the earth by his power; He has established the world by his wisdom and has stretched out the heavens by his discretion. (Revelation 1:8, Jeremiah 10:10, and Jeremiah 10:12)

He said in Isaiah: "Hast though not know? Hast thou not heard, [that] the everlasting God, the Lord, the Creator of the ends of the earth, fainteth not, neither is weary? [There is] no searching of his understanding" (Isaiah 40:28, NKJV).

What:

Growing in love with God is the understanding of his love for you. And the unfailing, untainted understanding that it can never and will never leave your presence. For God *so loved* the world that he gave his only son, that whoever believes in him should not perish but have everlasting life. No, in all of these things, we are more than conquerors through him who loved us. For I am that neither death nor life, nor angels nor rulers, nor things present nor things to come, nor powers, nor height nor depth, nor anything else in all creation, will be able to separate us from the love of God in Christ Jesus our Lord. But God, being rich in mercy, because of the great love with which he loved us, even when we were dead in our trespasses, made us alive together with Christ—by grace, you have been saved... The Lord your God is in your midst, a mighty one who will save; he will rejoice over you with gladness; he will quiet you by his love; he will exult over you with loud singing. (John 3:16, Romans 8:37–39, Ephesians 2:4–5, and Zephaniah 3:17)

When:

The moment I believe you may have started to grow in your love with him was right about the time when you realized he kept you in the midst of it all. You realized how much he has protected you and used what Satan meant for bad for his good. He worked so much out in your favor without desiring anything from you but a true relationship.

For me, it was around "Day Two: Defining Moments" when I stepped into the understanding that his love for me was inevitable, and my love for him was a huge part of me being sustained. Not just in my destiny, but in my daily life. (Psalms 34:17 and Hebrews 11:6) It awakened my spirit, bringing life back into me as I acknowledged him, saying, "Jesus, I'm in love with you! I need you, and I can't do any of this without you!"

Where:
It took place and residence in your heart! It's so real, and it's the realest love you can ever embrace and take part in.

How:
The *how* you began to grow in love with God is parallel with your *when*. It's when you experienced and acknowledged his faithfulness to you, in spite of the you who was suffocating. His faithfulness to you was without you even fully knowing him, loving him, or even accepting him yet. It's you realizing you didn't have to do a thing to deserve it or even earn it. I had to ask myself: how could I *not* grow in love with his amazing presence that loves me unconditionally in spite of myself?

Why:
What is life without his unfailing, unwavering, untainted, limitless, selfless, sustaining, and breathtaking love? I was in a place where I didn't want anything else but to stand still until I woke up each and every single day, knowing that I was saturated in his true love. I need him; you need him, and we need him. When I look back on everything, I wouldn't have made it without him. He has been so faithful. Check your journal; you will see that it's all he has ever been, even in your doubt. He has been faithful.

Stop and Journal

#DAY21
#BEGINNINGTOGROWINLOVEWITHGOD

Grow: to arise or issue as a natural development from
an original happening, circumstance, or source.
Love: a profoundly tender, passionate affection for another person.
God: the one Supreme Being, the creator and ruler
of the Universe (Father, Son, and Holy Spirit)
(Google definitions of "grow," "love," and "God.")

JOURNAL #31: Write your own: who, what, when, where, how
and why. Just for you and Him.

Who:

What:

When:

Where:

How:

Why:

To grow in love with God is to naturally arise in a passionate affection for the one creator and ruler of the universe (God the
Father, Son, and Holy Ghost). In that, you're expressing how much
you really want to start living again. It's a reflection of you saying to
yourself: *I want to continue becoming a better me in destiny.* No longer
walking it alone but understanding the one who loved you into the

light of it all, which once, to you, looked like the thickest darkness. You are here; you are still standing, and that means more than anything else in the world. There is destiny on your life. I know this because if there wasn't, you wouldn't have made it this far into *The 30-Day Journey to Loving the Woman in You.*

DAY 22

Learning How to Grow in Love with Me

Who can find a virtuous woman? For her price is far above rubies. She girdeth her loins with strength, and strengtheneth her arms.

—Proverbs 31:10, 17 (NKJV)

On day 22, you have to continue to remember, over anything and everything, that you are worth it. That's first, and it's because God says so. What God says lasts forever and ever, even past the end of (what we call) time. You are worth every bit of God's love, to be loved, and to give love freely, fearlessly, and without restraints. The key to this special day is *forgiveness*; forgiving yourself once and for all. Let it all go. The last bit of anything that has been keeping you reserved in life and even on this journey.

Let it go! The time is now! Let it go! What is your story without your flaws? You can't become the greater you without accepting, purging, and forgiving the *past* you! There is so much power in forgiveness, along with the greatest healing that you could ever experience. Tap into your truth, not anyone else's truth concerning you, but your truth so we can begin to take care of you like never before.

Stop and Journal

#DAY22
#LEARNINGHOWTOGROWINLOVEWITHME

"Who can find a virtuous woman? For her price is far above rubies.
She girdeth her loins with strength, and strengtheneth her arms."
(Proverbs 31:10,17 NKJV)

Take a look in the mirror, and within your own timing say,
"I love you so much and I forgive you, so I
can finally become the true you!"
Go! Go do it!
Take a moment, drop this book, and decree it to yourself!
Now, breathe!

JOURNAL #32: Write what you felt in this very moment.

1. What was your emotion?

2. What did you see leave?

3. What did you see come to life again?

You are worth it, and there will never be another day
where you don't live like you are worth every bit of His
greatness that He has placed on the inside of you.

"She perceiveth that her merchandise is good:
her candle goeth not out by night."
(Proverbs 31:18 NKJV)

The process began...

Remember this moment; record it if you have to and never ever,
ever, ever forget it. "Growing in Love with Me" is a day-to-day process of being consistent in how you feel, choosing to matter to your-

self like never before. Even in the moments when it doesn't make sense to put yourself first, you have to—without apology. It takes courage to love yourself past the past and into the truth of the present as you begin to live out your future…being the real, authentic, whole, healed, and free you.

There is only one you.

Remember that. Only you can be the best you there is.

This process I keep speaking of are steps to genuinely loving yourself, no longer apologizing for it. The way I apologized for loving myself was by dumbing down and not walking boldly in my greatness that God had entrusted me with. In that, I was apologizing for the intricate details that God had created when he had birthed me. To apologize about that to God is like slapping him in the face and saying, "What you made, Lord, is not enough. It's not great. You made a mistake in choosing me for such a calling because I'm just little old me. What you made isn't perfect in or out of destiny. You were wrong, Lord."

This may look like it's super dramatic, but it's so true in every way if you think about what we continually do to ourselves outside of God's beautiful will for our authentic self and life. Saying those words quoted above, to the Holy and Mighty One, who is all knowing and makes no mistakes…with a love for you that is sustaining, never failing, untainted, unconditional and forever present was mind blowing to me. When I realized the self-sabotaging damage I did to myself, I noticed something greater in that exact same moment. God loved me and saw me in the way I was always meant to be seen. In that, I put a halt to it all. I looked at myself in the mirror, with tears running down my eyes and said, "You are worth it, and there will never be another day where you don't live like you are worth every bit of his greatness that he has placed on the inside of you."

> She perceiveth that her merchandise is good: her candle goeth not out by night. (Proverbs 31:18, NKJV)

When you begin to grow in love with yourself after you understand the process that took place with you growing in *love with God,* you become limitless. There is no more "I can't," but your life instead becomes defined by: *"I can, and I will."*

There are certain steps it takes to growing in love with yourself, the right way, to where it never fails, even in the darkest seasons of our lives. This includes how you start to truly love people the right way. Before I take you through the steps, let me share something very key with you that helped me grow authentically in love with myself: in forgiving myself and on my journey to loving myself, I had to learn how to stop trying to predict and control my destiny. I needed to *simply surrender to everything.*

> She stretches out her hand to the poor; yea she reacheth forth her hands to the needy. Strength and honour are her clothing; and she shall rejoice in time to come. (Proverbs 31:20,25, NKJV)

I asked myself, "What is life if I can't be an amazing, authentic me to God, myself, and all of those around me?" I had to come to grips with the fact that I would never be perfect, and I was never meant to be. God is forever and always building and perfecting me; that's the beauty of living and how it is and has always been meant to be. It was never my job to create a perfect me but to *just be!* I threw up my hands and said, "God, help me to love myself enough to surrender to you, wholeheartedly casting out all fear with your love for me."

Stop and Journal

JOURNAL #33: Five steps you take to grow in love with yourself:

1. Honesty and truth: with God first, yourself second, and others third.

2. Forgiveness: through God first, for yourself second, and others third,

3. Restoration: in God first, within yourself second, and letting go of others third,

4. Acceptance of who God says you are.

5. Affirmations to write down and speak over yourself day in and day out.

These are steps to be repeated continually, in order to stay free to just be!

> She openeth her mouth with wisdom; and in her tongue is the law of kindness. (Proverbs 31:26, KJV)

The journaling section may take a while, and that's okay, but you must—and I mean *must*—do it. Let me explain why. When you're filling in the details of steps one through five, and speaking them out loud, you are releasing the hold that the enemy had on you and breaking yourself free from the bondage of the old you. It's truly allowing Jesus to come in and take away every scar and wound as if it never existed—the old scars—and the ones that are still to come.

Through these steps, we are deciding to no longer allow any wound or scar to stay longer than needed. Yes, it can all make us better, stronger, wiser, and builds a great story, but why not start choosing to have a story to where God's hand is moving continually through it all? No longer us standing in the way of his perfect will.

To where he gets every bit of glory because it's so good that even an unbeliever has to begin to say, "God did that for her."

> Many daughters have done virtuously, but thou excellest them all. (Proverbs 31:29, KJV)

Lastly, on day twenty-two, *no more settling!* In all that you have read and pressed through on this special day, understand that knowing who you are and whose you are is the most important factor to living, and living life more abundantly. As my pastor, Touré Roberts, of One Church International said, "I am what I am, by the grace of God! You can't possess and own who you are when you allow who you have been to disqualify you for who you are called by God to become! It's false humility to shrink and be less than. It's wrong to the one who created you and made you to just be you!"

Be the one who God can trust in and out of what you were labeled as before, and even now because what the world has to say means nothing when our father in Heaven has spoken into fruition all that you are and have always been meant and created to be.

> Favour is deceitful, and beauty is vain: but a woman that feareth the Lord, she shall be praised. Give her of the fruit of her hands; and let her own works praise her in the gates. (Proverbs 31:30–31)

Just be you, authentically and unapologetically!

DAY 23

Unconditionally Loving Others

Unconditional: not subject to any conditions.
"Unconditional surrender"
Synonyms: wholehearted, unqualified, unreserved,
unlimited, unrestricted, unmitigated, unquestioning.
Love: "Love is patient, love is kind. It does not envy, it does
not boast, it is not proud. (1 Corinthians 4:4, NIV)

On day 23, you're challenged with the understanding that you have to unconditionally begin to love others beyond what they have ever done to you and beyond what you've been put through…beyond any wounds or scars that you were just set free from. You have to go to that place of understanding that loving them as you've learned to love God and love yourself is just as important as any other form of love. Unconditionally loving others is true symbolism of fully being whole, healed, and free, in and out of destiny.

It doesn't matter if anybody can do anything for you; if they have committed the worse crime; if they're at the highest level of the government, or the lowest level of the streets in your city, you are called to choose to love and to love not matter what because someone needs it—just like you did and still do. There comes a point in life where you have to stand on the promises of what you have always desired and give that back in return, one hundred fold.

So if you have always desired to be loved, what's keeping you from loving others? You know you need it, so you know they need it. The price has been paid and the consequences have been done already. Choose to love. Choose to be the one people can say this about: "When I was in her presence, I felt loved." It doesn't matter if they know your name or not; it matters that they know when you walk in the room and will know what it feels like to be loved. To me, there is no other way to live.

At times, my greatest gift of loving others became one of my greatest downfalls. I loved people so much to the point of being wounded. I neglected the pain of the wound, and I still chose to love but then left a lot of mess for God to clean up on the inside of me. So in that, in loving others unconditionally, guard your heart and set boundaries.

> It does not dishonor others, it is not self-seeking, it is not easily angered, it keeps no records of wrongs. (1 Corinthians 4:5, NIV)

You can love people limitlessly and unconditionally and still have boundaries so you don't have to go through what you've been through before. Loving others unconditionally doesn't mean becoming dumb and allowing the same things to occur over and over again. Loving people unconditionally says: "I want to love them with the love of the Lord. I want them to know that they matter in this world, but not at the cost of my self-worth and self-love." Guard your heart; protect it, nurture it, and cultivate it as God has asked you to. Set boundaries and know who's with and who's for you—just for you—not for what you can do for them, and not for how far they feel you can take them.

Know who your true friends are, know who your assignments are, and know who your "destiny mates" are. There's a big difference.

This is where setting your boundaries begins:

1. There may be some *friends* in your life who aren't destiny mates, but they are your friends. They support you, stand by you, believe in you, pray for you, and help nurture your atmosphere but have nothing to do with the destiny that's inside of you. They simply help with pouring into the person walking out the destiny.

2. Then you have the ones who are *assignments*: they are not for you to vent to, for you to go to with your issues, or for you to have as an open ear. No! Through God and only God, you are that for them. You're their wisdom and strength, and you're the one God has called to help keep them lifted up through any and every season and circumstance until he says the time is up. An assignment is strictly from God. Don't make someone an *assignment* if they're not supposed to be. Don't make someone your *best friend* if they're not supposed to be and don't make someone your *destiny-mate* if they were never intended to be.

3. A *destiny-mate* is someone who is assigned to the movement of God on the inside of you, the kingdom expansion, and the bringing of God's kingdom in heaven to his kingdom on this earth. It's the power that you have on the inside of you, and that they have on the inside of them to walk through this thing together, pressing each other forward, believing in each other, speaking life into each other, and staying consistent in your daily walks as you are taking your time in reading God's Word. Those are *destiny-mates*!

"Love does not delight in evil but rejoices with the truth." (1 Corinthians 4:6, NIV)

In all of that, know who is there for *a reason, a season,* or *a lifetime.* There's a big difference, and in knowing that, in tapping into that, and being in tune with that, it will be so much easier for you to love others unconditionally. You will know where each person in your life belongs, and you won't expect anything more from them than exactly what they are called to, concerning you.

Stop and Journal

#DAY23
#UNCONDITIONALLYLOVINGOTHERS

Unconditional: Not subject to any conditions.
"Unconditional surrender."
Synonyms: wholehearted, unqualified, unreserved,
unlimited, unrestricted, unmitigated, unquestioning.

(Google definition of "unconditional.")

Love
"Love is patient, love is kind. It does not envy,
it does not boast, it is not proud."
(1 Corinthians 4:4 NIV)

JOURNAL #34: Write these down in spirit and in truth.

1.   Make a list of your closest friends:
2.   Make a list of those you feel are an assignment:
3.   Make a list of those you believe are your destiny-mates
     (Like Elizabeth and Mary, the ones who are called to help
     you birth the greatest vision of your life.):

"…trusts, always hopes, always perseveres."
(1 Corinthians 4:7 NIV)

Believe it or not…
You are free in this very moment to love again, only
in, with, and through God's love this time.

As you make those lists in your journal, pray over them and seek
God in understanding. Is everyone where they belong, or is there
a need for some rearranging? When you open up the way for God
to be able to tell you who's what and so on, you save yourself a lot
of heartache. You actually keep yourself in a safe place. That's what
makes unconditional love so much more breathtaking because you
are able to do it from a healthy place, a secure place, a knowing place,

instead of a tainted, unknowing, false expectations, and assumptions type of space. As you begin to learn who you are and whose you are, it's going to become so much easier to know who is and who isn't your future, your present, and your purpose. That right there is everything. Absolutely everything.

> Trusts, always hopes, always perseveres. (1 Corinthians 4:7, NIV)

Challenge: put yourself in a position that you have to love on someone you don't know or may have just met. Go to a place you have never gone before and tell someone, "I love you!" Tell someone they matter; tell someone that Jesus loves them. Do something that you've never done before so you can begin to be a part of the movement to change this world through God's love.

Practice an unfailing love, an unconditional love...a love that may not make any sense to some people, and a love that literally can help set the captives free. Less people being killed and less lives being lost, all because you may have told someone that you love them, or that Jesus loves them. They may have never heard those three words ever, in their entire lives. Be wise but have so much wisdom that you tap into a place for someone that they have never been.

Place yourself in the atmosphere where you're needed and not just wanted. To where you can be that true essence of God's love, genuinely, whole-heartedly, and from the purest of places that there has ever been; where you awaken something on the inside of someone so they never wake up a day again, not knowing if they are loved or otherwise. So they can say that they are loved because of your obedience to God in showing his unconditional, unwavering, unlimited love.

Believe it or not...

You are free,

In this very moment,

To love again,

Only in, with, and through

God's love

This time.

DAY 24

Lean Not unto Thy Own Understanding

*Trust in the Lord with all thine heart and lean
not unto thine own understanding, In all thy ways
acknowledge him and He shall direct your path.*

—Proverbs 3:5–6 (KJV)

On day 24, you must step into the most vulnerable place you probably have ever been before. Take the blame, shame, burdens, and weight off. Do it! Just take it all off and chuck it as far as you can. It does not belong to you; God wants it all, each and every day. It was never meant for you to carry, period! When you do this, mean it with all your might and heart. Don't play with it, or your emotions because that's what caused all of this. You were consistently taking things on again and again after you had just cleaned up so much of the mess that had you suffocating from the past.

Part two of this journey is not about becoming perfect and everything becoming cupcakes and ice cream. It's about being able to handle things the right way when similar situations occur again and again. Everything comes full circle in life at least three or more times, and you must continue mastering the ultimate kill of that deadly cycle. It's trying to keep you from being great, which is keeping you from being you!

Stop and Journal

#DAY24
#LEANNOTUNTOTHYOWNUNDERSTANDING

"Trust in the Lord with all thine heart and lean
not unto thine own understanding, in all thy ways
acknowledge him and He shall direct your path."
(Proverbs 3:5-6 KJV)

JOURNAL #35: Create your own circle diagram:

It's time to break every chain!

In this area of our lives, we will constantly be attacked over and over again, but we have to learn how to surrender once and for all so the load becomes light. This happens when we begin to grow through it and stay solid on our foundation of peace, joy, and faith that only God has given us—in that alone. Stay in a place of understanding that it's not about you in the thick of it; it's about you overcoming all of it.

The stronger you become, the more hits you will get, but it's up to you to decide if they will keep affecting you or just bounce off the shield covering you. You must continually say, "God, here I am again. Have your way, Lord. I am yours, not my own. Have your way, Lord!" It's our choice to receive the *set-ups* of the enemy or the *"bless-ups"* from God. Think about this: can you actually lean on yourself in the natural/physical? No!

So why do we continue to try to figure it all out on our own, in the natural and spiritual realm? It's because, once again, we have *trust issues*. In that, you step into that place of fear, believing that the same outcome from last time will be the same one this time. But it won't if you let go and allow God to step in and protect you from that thing that could be detrimental to you and your destiny. Some of you may be like me—hard headed—trying to handle it all on your own. But that's not for this part of your journey. This must die!

It was stated so clearly on day twenty-three that love equals trust, and trust equals love. I realized that if God trusts my imperfect self so much, why couldn't I trust him in all of his perfect ways? Living with *trust issues* is dangerous because we don't know even a quarter of what God knows concerning our present and our future.

If we want to be honest, we know *nada*! So how can we really lean on our own anything when we actually don't know a thing, except for what we have lived so far? Even so, we made decisions based off of feeling and what we thought. But in actuality, we still didn't experience the fullness of the greatness in any of those situations because we chose our will over God's. I'm only speaking on what I've lived. At times, we do so much damage to our families, others, and our own God-Given destinies when we live without God being allowed to be the potter of his clay and masterpiece, which is you!

In all of this, I'm going to tell you again as the Lord told me:
Just be!
Just be!
Even when you don't know what it all looks like!
Just be!
In every moment of your life,
Just be!
During your triumphs and your downfalls,
Just be!
When your joy is so sound,
Just be!
When your anger is raging,
Just be!
When nothing makes since,
Just be!
When everything that could go wrong goes wrong,
Just be!
When everything is going right and it's easy to smile,

Just be!
When you have to sit in silence and let the tears fall,
Just be!
When you are standing at the top of a mountain, looking at all you have overcome,
Just be!
When have God's peace that surpasses all understanding,
Just be!
When you are no longer afraid to shine your light,
Just be!
When you press past everything that tried to break you,
Just be!
When you are on your knees in your secret place,
Just be!
When you need all of heaven to back you up,
Just be!
When you can finally say, "I'm more than okay, and I am loving myself,"
Just be!
When you've done all you can, just stand and continue to
Just be!
When you start to see yourself through God's eyes,
Just be!
When everyone is saying you should be married by now,
Just be!
When you are in waiting for God's perfect timing,
Just be!
When God speaks a word to the depths of your spirit, heart, and soul,
Just be!
Worship, worship, worship, and
Just be!
When you are stepping into destiny,
Just be!
When God is birthing your journey for His glory,
Just be!

It's only in Him, through Him, and with Him that you will be able to

Just be!

Stop and Journal

JOURNAL #36: Define "just be for yourself and your destiny!

JUST BE!

You are almost there, beloved. Take a deep breath and prepare for the final blueprints that God has designed for you so you can become who you were always meant to be. You are worth every bit of this journey, and as you start leaning upon God instead of yourself, you will begin to understand what true living, loving, and joy feels like each and every day. Come on...you are almost there! You are almost there!

DAY 25

I Am More than Enough

Being confident of this very thing, that He who has begun a good work in you will complete it until the day of Jesus Christ.

—Philippians 1:6 (NIV)

On day 25, I had to stop and take a moment of reconciliation with myself from day one to day twenty-four and say, "Thank you!" I wasn't finding myself saying, "I'm sorry," anymore. I was boldly and unapologetically saying, "Thank you," to who I was, to who I am, and to who I am becoming every day. I began to fall in love with myself through God's love. I am in a place of understanding what it means to be more than enough for God, this world, my destiny, and the deepest, most important part of it all: myself. I asked myself: *what does it all look like?*

What does being *more than enough* feel like, speak like, live like, and walk like? It's you just being you! In love with yourself, the way God is in love with you. Just being as you are choosing to be whole, healed, and free as you step into your destiny. No longer being moved by any transgression or broken promise, but realizing that God keeping his promises to you, and you keeping your own promises to you is more than enough. Knowing what God sees when he looks at you and no longer questioning how he feels about you! You are here, so you matter. We matter. Others matter.

The scripture at the beginning of this chapter says so much in just one sentence, and it is a promise that will never go void or fall by the wayside. You are so important to God that he birthed, anointed, and appointed people to transcribe scriptures like this so that on a good or not so good day, you always have something so solid to stand on. It's something that is unchanging and never fails to be all that he has designed it to be—just for you! We live in a world where people like us one day, and the next, try to take our gig, our man, or our identity. God already knew that, so he wanted us to always know that we meant something to someone greater than ourselves and greater than the people surrounding us.

So with all of the things the world may throw at us, we won't be shaken because every promise ever needed to step into destiny has been laid out and defined in his true and living Word, which is the same yesterday, today, and forever. Take a moment and go through your journal and look at some of the scriptures—those included by me and maybe those added in by you. In doing this, you are going to see not only how much he loves you, but also see the ultimate factor in proclaiming in his strength, "I am more than enough."

I am more than enough...

> He came so he could see what it would feel like to be you.
> We cannot add to him nor diminish him. He is God all by himself but maybe we can learn something from a baby in a manger. Leave your perspective long enough to see someone else's, see their pain and the way they grew up and see that they didn't get there by themselves. (Bishop T. D. Jakes's podcast, "For Unto Us" Sermon, 12/21/2014)

Can you—just as I had to—take this word and speak it to yourself? Leave your perspective long enough to see your past pain, the way you grew up, and come to realize that God was with you every step of the way.

He kept me,

I am more than enough!

He held me,

I am more than enough!
He heard my cry,
I am more than enough!
He sustained me,
I am more than enough!
He healed me,
I am more than enough!
He removed that bullet,
I am more than enough!
He restored my marriage,
I am more than enough!
He took the abuser and the abuse away,
I am more than enough!
He challenged me to be better and do better,
I am more than enough!
He didn't let me fall,
I am more than enough!
He carried me through the fire,
I am more than enough!
He protected me from Satan's plan,
I am more than enough!
He saved me from the broke me,
I am more than enough!
He has my husband in waiting, being prepared for me,
I am more than enough!
He turned it all around for my family,
I am more than enough!
He is turning it around for me,
I am more than enough!
He heard my prayers and answered in His time,
I am more than enough!
He paid every bill,
I am more than enough!
He didn't let me die,
I am more than enough!
He accepted me when others rejected me,

I am more than enough!
He danced with me when I thought I was all alone,
I am more than enough!
He sits with me, listens to me, cherishes me,
I am more than enough!
He never gets tired or weary of me,
I am more than enough!
I am, because He is!
In that alone,
I am more than enough!
I am here says,
I am more than enough!
He is with me never to leave me or forsake me
And continues to forgive me,
I am more than enough!
He waits for me even in my darkest seasons,
I am more than enough!
He sees me beyond me,
I am more than enough!
He has made provision for me in all things,
I am more than enough!
He believes in me,
I am more than enough!
He taught me to believe in me,
I am more than enough!
I can do all things through Christ Jesus who strengthens me,
I am more than enough!
No weapon formed against me shall ever prosper,
I am more than enough!
I am more than enough!

Stop and Journal

#DAY25
#IAMMORETHANENOUGH

"Being confident of this very thing, that He who has begun a
good work in you will complete it until the day of Jesus Christ;"
(Philippians 1:6 NIV)

Take a listen:
http://www.lightsource.com/ministry/the-potters-
house/its-not-what-it-looks-like-435123.html
Bishop T.D. Jakes' podcast "For Unto Us" sermon, 12/21/2014

JOURNAL #37: Write your personal "I am more than enough"
statements to you! I am more than enough!

"But you are a chosen race, a royal priesthood, a
holy nation, a people for his own possession, that
you may proclaim the excellencies of him who called
you out of darkness into his marvelous light."
(1 Peter 2:9 NIV)

And since Christ is married to the church, he explains that knowing
you is needed in order to dwell with you. He came so he could see what
it's like to be you. Being exhausted would not have been experienced by
him without him coming. Without him coming, sleep would have been
foreign. Because in his eternal state, he neither sleeps nor slumbers. It's
why, at two o'clock in the morning when you begin to pray, you don't
have to wake him up. Your two o'clock is someone else's eleven a.m. He
can't go to bed due to your night being someone else's day. He is available
to you all the time. And he came so he would know what being lonely
or empty or temptation was. He came so that he could understand what
it's like to be you. It's about him being a God that is so in love with you.
He is willing to see your world from your perspective…

When you are trying to pray, He will understand
what you are trying to say! (Bishop T. D. Jakes
Podcast "For unto Us" Sermon 12/21/2014)

This is how in love with you God is. He always has been and always will be!

You are more than enough,
I am more than enough,
Others are more than enough,
We are all more than enough!
Decree and declare that it is so!
In Jesus's name, amen!

> But you are a chosen race, a royal priesthood, a holy nation, a people for his own possession, that you may proclaim the excellencies of him who called you out of darkness into his marvelous light. (1 Peter 2:9, NIV)

DAY 26

Who Am I That You Are Mindful of Me

What is man that you are mindful of him, and the son of man, that you care for him?

—Psalms 8:4 (ESV)

On day 26, you wake up realizing that there has been another shift. A shift that is a bit drastic yet subtle within your spirit, heart, and soul that the grace of God has established you in. The beautiful art of humility has taken reign in you acknowledging that your absolute, best days are ahead in you being authentically you. You have been shaped, pruned, plucked up, and planted over and over again with "the joy of the Lord being your strength" (Nehemiah 8:10 NIV).

By this day, you have truly allowed yourself to be captured by the heart of God, knowingly, and enjoying the process of what that feels like. You are an extension of him, as you read yesterday. He sent his son so that there would no longer be a misunderstanding on our end. He will always understand our functioning and developing stages of *becoming*. I can honestly say that I've never felt him ever so present than in my days writing this book and during my process of loving myself authentically and genuinely.

I must tell you this small yet life-changing story. Believe me when I say that your life and destiny is truly about God using you for his glory.

In the second week of January, right after I had started back working as a choreographer on the new faith-based musical film, *Revival,* I was searching for a place that could turn my videotapes from my "DANCE 2 LIVVV Master Class Tour" into DVDs. I went to one place that didn't provide such services, but one of their employees knew a place that did.

He explained, "There is a mom and pop shop I went to, years ago, in Burbank. I'm not sure if it is still there, but you could try." He vaguely remembered where it was located. I thanked him over and over again, left the store with two street names and was able to find the digital/photo lab place. When I went inside, I met the owner, Ray, a sixty-eight-year-old Armenian, softhearted man. He had so much joy and helped me out immediately. I couldn't stop worshipping God for this answered prayer.

So a few days went by, and I went in to the store again with an amazing little dancer I mentor, Erin. While she went to grab food, I walked into the shop to see Ray there with his eyes so wide and heart so open. He asked me, "What do you do?" I explained to him my calling and career and what I've stepped into for the Kingdom of God to be glorified through all forms of the Arts and Entertainment. As I explained, he had tears coming down his face said to me, "I had the best time in Jesus this past Sunday; better than any church service I have attended. It was from seeing just two minutes of one of your videotapes. Can you teach me how to dance with my Jesus?"

I began to cry, and he said, "What you have done and are doing with those children, youth, and adults has changed my life forever. I love Jesus so much, and I want to dance with him like you taught those beautiful children to dance with him and for him. This world needs you. I need you. Jesus needs you, and those children need you. Promise me you will never stop what you are doing."

He continued, asking, "Can you do something for me? Can you pray for me? I feel like I'm losing hope. I want you to pray for me, any time you think of me."

With tears falling even more, I asked him if I could pray with him right then.

He answered, "My God. Please! Yes, please!"

I grabbed his hands and prayed a prayer from the Father's heart beyond what I even knew was going on in this man's life. God began to breathe new life into this amazing soul, and as I ended in, "It is done, it is well, and it is finished, in Jesus's name, amen," I hugged him, and he wept profusely. I told him not to ever give up, to always know that God loves him so much and has him in his hands.

As Erin walked in during the prayer, she began to cry also and heard his heart cry out for restoration and peace. Ray then said to Erin, "You stay connected to her; don't allow her to give up or stop changing lives for God's kingdom, including yours. We need her. We need what you guys are doing—to help change this world." He turned to me, still weeping and said, "I will be praying for you; you changed my life forever. I want to attend your church. Please keep in touch with me whenever you think about me. We need you; you have a gift."

"I know God hasn't forgotten about me and still loves me because he brought you to me. You are an angel, and I will worship him every day for this moment. I never stopped believing in my Jesus, but I know now more than ever that he is here, holding me, keeping me, and sustaining me. Thank you, Reyna, for coming to me from Jesus and restoring my love for him and my faith in him. I am forever grateful. Please never stop. God has so much more coming toward you because he can trust you to do his work."

God is forever so mindful of us, and we are never forgotten in any season of our lives. In the midst of God resurrecting his presence in Ray's life that day, he affirmed me in my calling, destiny, and importance of my obedience to funding my own tour for him, all by faith. I am just a vessel. We are just vessels. Ultimately, it's not about us; we simply receive the blessings of what our obedience and alignment does to the hearts of this nation and world. What seems so small to someone else is actually saving lives, restoring hope, and sustaining faith for millions of others.

How has God shown you that he is mindful of you, and what you are capable of doing for his kingdom, for his glory?

Stop and Journal

#DAY26
#WHOAMITHATYOUAREMINDFULOFME

"What is man that you are mindful of him, and
the son of man, that you care for him?"
(Psalms 8:4 ESV)

JOURNAL #38: Write your story, because you have one, too.

Life to the Just:

> I will stand upon my watch, and set me upon
> the tower, and will watch to see what he will say
> unto me, and what I shall answer when I am
> reproved. Behold, his soul which is lifted up is
> not upright in him: But the just shall live by his
> faith. (Habakkuk 2:1,4, KJV)

As he is mindful of you, begin to be even more mindful of others
so they can finally step into their God-Ordained destiny. Someone
is depending on you to make it so they can finally believe that they
were called, destined, and chosen to make it too.

It's in you, beloved…It's in you!

DAY 27

The Secret Place

He that dwelleth in the secret place of the most High
shall abide under the shadow of the Almighty.

—Psalms 91:1 (KJV)

On day 27, you tuck yourself away. You tuck yourself completely away and sustain yourself in knowing that this is the beginning of you truly, and completely, never being the same. It's a beautiful time that you must grab hold of, without feeling guilty for it or indecisive about it. This could mean taking a *stay-cation:* a vacation without traveling; staying in a hotel or a secret place, away from everyone. Others can know you are gone, but just not quite sure where. No cell phone, e-mails, work…nada!

The beauty of this time is that you get to accept the *now* as you step into the new, refined, and limitless you! This now moment is understanding that the next phase, probably the most important day of *The 30-Day Journey*, is vital to you truly being whole beyond what you have ever experienced in your entire life. You are so liberated to the point that you stand on the promise of being free in just being. This space of living is in that special, *secret place.*

You have an appointment with your Heavenly father to rest in him and listen to his heart concerning his love for you. This is where you open up your heart to receive the true, living, and sustaining words that will execute the next phase of your life, affectively, and expeditiously. Yes, I know this may sound impossible as you think of everything you have to do, and all the people you have to cater

150

to, but let me help you understand what God did to help make me understand. If you don't take this day, time, weekend, or week to detox and allow yourself to be poured into by the only one who knows you better than yourself, you could miss it—miss the most important, defining moment of becoming you!

If you miss that, you've taken these twenty-seven days of *The 30-Day Journey* all in vain. No dramatics, no bluffing, no overanalyzing. Think about it for a second. If you can't give yourself one day alone in that secret place, with just you and your Heavenly father, you've missed it all. This is probably one of the most symbolic moments and days of understanding what it truly means to love yourself and be in love with the new you. *The you* God has revealed and is continually developing you into. You've come too far. So...

There is a decision that has to be made before we go any further. It's the same decision I had to make when I was ready. But me waiting until I was ready was almost too late within the timeline of what God was doing expeditiously, concerning my destiny. Trust! That was what I was lacking and needed in order to surrender to, whole-heartedly and continually. It was and is the key, to this day, in just allowing yourself to be. It's trust. Trust God, yourself, the process, and what is about to take place in your secret place in him.

> I will say of the Lord, He is my refuge and my fortress: my God; in him will I trust. (Psalms 91:2, KJV)

You can do this!

Stop and Journal

#DAY27
#THESECRETPLACE

"He that dwelleth in the secret place of the most High shall abide under the shadow of the Almighty."
(Psalms 91:1 KJV)

"Stay-cation: A vacation without traveling; staying in a hotel or a secret place away from everyone with them knowing you are gone, but just not quite sure where. No cell phone, emails, work…nada!"

You can do this!

JOURNAL #39: Pick one of the two options:

(circle one)

1. I am packing a bag and taking myself to my secret place.

2. I am staying here and not going a step further on this journey until I am ready to get to my secret place.

(After you choose, begin to write and explain why you chose the option that you did.)

If you chose option two: Please stop here!

"Because thou hast made the Lord, which is my refuge,
even the most High, thy habitation; there shall no evil befall
thee, neither shall any plague come nigh thy dwelling."
(Psalms 91:9-10 KJV)

Even when everything is telling you *no*, you must fight for your *yes*! The enemy will always try to sabotage your growth into the next phase, especially when it comes to the point of being alone with God to receive your healing, freedom, and destiny blueprint. As you learned before, it's never in your own strength that you overcome, nor is it in your own strength that you can take yourself away from the noise into the silence. Trust me, beloved queens, I know. I fought and I won. What's your verdict going to be?

> Surely he shall deliver thee from the snare of the fowler, and from the noisome pestilence. He shall cover thee with his feathers, and under his wings shalt thou trust: his truth shall be thy shield and buckler. (Psalms 91:3–4, KJV)

So for those who chose option number two in the journal, please stop here until you are ready to be tucked away from it all. In that, I honor you for being honest with yourself and not moving forward falsely. But I'm also praying you don't wait too long before certain doors are out of your hands' reach. What doors are you willing to let close, due to the fear of just being? Please stop here!

For those who chose option number one in the journal, pack your bag, grab this book and your journal, get in your car, and head to your divine destination called "The Secret Place." This is when you tell yourself that you matter more than anyone else's needs right now, and your destiny depends on it. Being alone with God is probably the most incredible choice you could've ever made for yourself.

> Because thou hast made the Lord, which is my refuge, even the most High, thy habitation; there shall no evil befall thee, neither shall any plague come nigh thy dwelling. (Psalms 91:9–10, KJV)

Now that you have arrived and settled in, I humbly say, "Thank you from the depth of my heart because you are worth this time and moment in him to be sustained in becoming the true you! If only you knew what is about to be birthed in you, through you, and with you from this time in him and with him."

Picture this time as the woman with the issue of blood, who had more faith than anyone who Jesus had encountered. As she pressed passed the crowds and touched the hem of his garment, she was healed immediately by her faith as he felt all power being pulled from him.

Your secret place is her touch of his garment. It's by your faith, beloved. Do you understand now why the trust and faith was needed in your rest since day one? Without one, the other will fail. All three work together in destiny, in your bond with God, and in becoming whole, healed, and free in order to step into destiny, limitlessly, for eternity.

> For he shall give his angels charge over thee, to keep thee in all thy ways. They shall bear thee up in their hands, lest thou dash thy foot against a stone. (Psalms 91:11–12, KJV)

Stop and Journal

JOURNAL #40: Write your transparent answers down to each question.

1. How do you feel in this very moment?

2. What is your heart saying to your soul?

3. Are you open to receive what's about to happen?

4. What do you desire to do next in your secret place?

The secret place is just for you; no one else but you. Personally, God gave me no other option but to simply sit and just be in his presence, so I didn't miss one thing that he desired and needed to share with me. The revelations were pertaining to his promises and the millions of lives assigned to me. It started here for me, right here. During my time was when the blueprint of *The 30-Day Journey to*

Loving the Woman in Me was birthed. So for you, in this very moment you can do whatever you want: talk, listen, cry, meditate, scream, smile, laugh, sing, dance, write, paint, watch a movie, worship, rest, and really rest—or even just be still in being authentically you.

It's your time, beloved! This is the safest place you could ever be. No one and nothing can come up against you, unless you allow it to do so. In the secret place, take a second and know that in this very moment, you are free to be. When it's all said and done, there will be a finishing work completed in your healing process, and the love that you will have unconditionally for you in and out of time, seasons, and in worry or worship, will be breathtaking. You will feel the truth in what it means to feel and know that you are more than enough. The authority that you will now have will begin to transform your way of life. Mark my words: there is no failure in God. With fear being demolished, there is nothing being fed to defeat your stance, but only feeding the greater you in this special, secret place!

Your territory has just been expanded.

Trust the process.

It's already done, in Jesus's name, amen.

> Thou shalt tread upon the lion and adder: the young lion and the dragon shalt thou trample under feet. Because he hath set his love upon me, therefore will I deliver him: I will set him on high, because he hath known my name. He shall call upon me, and I will answer him: I will be with him in trouble; I will deliver him, and honour him. With long life will I satisfy him, and shew him my salvation. (Psalms 91:13–16, KJV)

He is a God who could never lie, and this is his promise to you and me.

For those who chose option two, when you have decided to go away to your secret place, get there and begin to journal as you read this chapter. Saturate yourself in the fullness of what it looks like to love yourself more than you ever have before.

DAY 28

I Am Me

Stunning and radiant as the sun that sets over the sea,
just being as I am in His presence, forever
and always, I am free as I am me.

On day 28, you have come back from one of the most fulfilling times in your life. You may still be there, and it's one of the most dynamic moments captured in time and space. Your secret place was redefined to you in the right way, without compromising anything concerning this newly-positioned you in his love and your love for yourself. "I am me!" That says so much in itself, but what does it mean *to you*?

Stop and Journal

#DAY28
#IAMME

"Stunning and radiant as the sun that sets over the sea, just being as I am in His presence forever and always, I am free as I am me."

JOURNAL #41: "I am me..." (Define what this means to you, in any way you feel led, and write it down.)

What I developed in this season was that "I am me." *Me* is defined solely in God's love and joy that he gives to me so willingly and freely to share with every single person around me. I had to vow to God and myself that I would no longer apologize for being free in knowing that I am me, authentically and breathtakingly. I am me in him, and without him, I am nothing.

God took me to a place where I began to pick up the pieces of myself. Pieces that were never meant to leave my presence. Pieces that created my authenticity. It was mind blowing to recognize all the things I had stopped doing or limited myself in becoming; all because they weren't what others wanted or desired in me or from me. Hold on tight; this gets a little more real than any moment on this entire journey.

The Lord took me down a secret path that was stunning; with colors of life as restoration was rightfully present in each step taken. He began to tell me what to put back on and take back because it had always been mine to begin with. They were certain things I had released or stopped doing. They were things that God had never desired for me to leave behind. And they were things that ultimately completed the essence of who I am to him:

1. Being quiet and reserved as I observed people as a child was wrong and disrespectful in many people's opinions. All I wanted was to be under my mommy and know that I was protected. As long as I was with her, I knew anything I said, even if it didn't matter to anyone else, mattered to her.

2. I quit track and field twice within twelve years of running. I loved it so much, but I never fit in anywhere with anyone. I was always left out and mistreated by the black girls, so I quit to make it peaceful and get away from the pain they kept inflicting on me.

3. I cut my hair short three times in my life, thinking it would ease the hate I received from one of my own race of women, or because the men I dated were with me for what I looked like instead of how pure my heart was. Yet I loved my hair

just the way it was and still never felt enough after the damage was done.

4. I tried so hard to make others feel better about themselves, to the point of dumbing myself down or allowing them to belittle me in their speech as much as possible. To make others comfortable, I would water down my gifts and anointing from God, just to keep friends and no longer stand out so they could. All of a sudden, acceptance meant everything.

5. I almost committed suicide three times: once at thirteen years old, once at twenty-three years old, and again at twenty-seven years old; because I felt that no matter what I did, I would never be enough. But I loved God and life so much. The weight of life and people's expectations became too much. My joy became dust.

6. The week of my graduation from college, I allowed the enemy to trick me into thinking the only way to have a great, lasting relationship, without my boyfriend cheating, was by having premarital sex. I was so tired of the past relationships failing because of what (I thought) I was saving for God, myself, and my future husband.

7. I began to say, "I'm no longer a dancer" due to something my acting agent had said to me a few years ago—that choosing to be an actress or dancer was necessary to step into the fullness of being an actress. But I had been doing both for years, and dancing had been my voice. At times, it was my only voice for years, from God to me and from me to him, this nation, and the world. Did God say I was done dancing?

8. Lastly, I lost my joy to use my gifts for God's kingdom when that was all I had ever prayed for. This was due to how some artists I have worked with saw the art, excellence, and my heart in my gift from God. They forget how it deserved to be compensated and not freely abused. It took me years to heal and understand that it wasn't God's fault at all. It was the wounded people doing what they

only knew how to do because of what had been done to them. I had to remember who I was working for, which was solely for his glory, not for mine or for others'. As long as God was being honored, glorified, and his kingdom consistently being expanded, my joy was full as my eyes were with tears.

I, even I, am he that blotteth out the transgressions for mine own sake, and will not remember thy sins. (Isaiah 43:25, KJV)

I'm weeping as I'm writing because this isn't even a quarter of the moments that many know. They tormented every inch of me just being. I realized that the most devastating thing was that my presence had been stolen from me in the most deceptive way since I was a child. The enemy had taken his time in constructing individuals and moments to break what had been so solid in the arms of God. God birthed me into this world from my mother's womb with the understanding that I would never be able to fulfill my sole purpose in life without him.

He created a dependency through me being born with clubfeet (what Satan meant for bad, God turned into our good) and trusting him as he guided me into overcoming probably the greatest struggle of my entire life. He built a relationship with me from the beginning, based all on faith and trust with love. The not knowing was what sustained, at one time, me, and now it's begun to sustain me again. I'm in a place of knowing he is God, all by himself. He has not failed me once or compromised his promises or words. It's the same for you! This I know, without even knowing you. How and why? Because you are still here!

I need you to catch this and realize the greatness on your life in moments like this that God has defined himself to you over and over again! Tune in and tap in really quick!

1. The attack against my quietness was used to bring out a bundle of joy and life that people began to always want

around them. It opened up the door for me to speak power into others and bring life to any atmosphere that I came into contact with. I broke free into what God would later use to encourage multitudes, including my own family, and even my enemies at times.

2. The rejection of my track and field peers threw me into the gift of dancing. When I no longer felt safe and was constantly wounded, God lit a fire within me to transition me into a position on a new level of being free in the art of dancing. He began a good and great work on the inside of me as he healed me.

3. Though I cut my hair for the wrong reasons, it helped me to realize that I am not my hair, and I am more than my beauty. I am a phenomenal woman with a heart that God uses to help set so many people free into their destinies, through his love and word. I began to be able to see myself beyond what was used to cover up my true essence.

4. God altered my way of thinking, and my perception shifted in the understanding that if I loved people as much as I always expressed, I would no longer dumb down myself for them to feel good. I would rise up higher so they would become uncomfortable with being complacent and rise to the leaders and world changers that were planted deep down within them. I began to shine so they could know and believe that it was okay to do so.

5. The three suicide attempts became a testimony that made me immediately relatable to people all over this nation and world. It gave me a new level of worship, surrender, and obedience to speaking life, even in the midst of death. I began to know when I had stepped into the presence of someone who was dying. I could call forth that spirit because I had dealt with it face to face, once upon a time. It built me up after I died to self and became alive in Christ like never before.

6. When I thought losing my virginity was the death of me, my submission to God after that fall brought the life of

restoration in who I was destined to step into as I was *becoming*. After losing what I was holding sacred for God, myself, and my future husband, I realized my worth more than ever before. At times, we don't realize how important or amazing something is until it's gone. Now I stand in knowing I am everything to God. Being pure is everything to me, in him. Now I'm in waiting for my king—my future husband.

7. My agent telling me my dancing was over was a set-up from the enemy, and a "bless-up" from God. In that moment and season, God spoke my FHG Entertainment company and brought my DANCE 2 LIVVV Master Class Tour into existence. He expanded my territory all over this nation, and now this world, through teaching the art, passion, love, and worship of dance in all styles to children and adults. I still dance but with a whole new anointing and level of understanding that this gift is not my own; it's to share with this nation and world to build a legacy for his glory forever and ever. Amen.

8. The greatest lesson in losing my joy is that I no longer mistakenly glorify others, but the creator of the souls who were used by God to help open doors seen and unseen. It was never them; it was him all along. My gratitude was simply: "I praise God for you and your obedience to his will for this project, and his vision to have me a part of it all! God gets all the glory!" I appreciate God for each of those people who were used by him and am forever humbled to live my God-Designed destiny!

Stop and Journal

JOURNAL #42: Write down your set-ups that became your victories, and then simply worship because He is so worthy of all your praise.

Read it this time with the mindset of: "I am me."
It is done...

Thou shall not be afraid for the terror by night; nor for the arrow that flieth by day; Nor for the pestilence that walketh in darkness; nor for the destruction that wasteth at noonday. A thousand shall fall at thy side and ten thousand at thy right hand; but it shall not come nigh thee. Only with thine eyes shalt though behold and see the reward of the wicked. Because thou hast made the Lord, which is my refuge, even the most High, thy habitations; There shall no evil befall thee, neither shall any plague come nigh thy dwelling. For he shall give his angels charge over thee, to keep thee in all thy ways. They shall bear thee up in their hands, lest thou dash thy foot against a stone. Thou shalt tread upon the lion and adder: the young lion and the dragon shalt thou trample under feet. Because he hath set his love upon me, therefore will I deliver him: I will set him on high, because he hath known my name. He shall call upon me, and I will answer him: I will be with him in trouble; I will deliver him, and honour him. With long life will I satisfy him, and shew him my salvation. (Psalms 91:5-16, KJV)

It is done.

DAY 29

Whole, Healed, And Free

And it is God who establishes us with you in Christ,
and has anointed us, and who has also put his seal
on us and given us his Spirit in our hearts as a guar-
antee. (2 Corinthians 1:21–22, ESV)

On day twenty-nine, you must come to the place of speaking over yourself, "I am whole, healed, and free." It's a declaration, not an assumption. It's a fact, not a hope. And it's your new truth, no longer a false representation of you. It is you because, finally, you *are*. There's no need to even look back; because the proof isn't in the *then*, it's in the *now* as you look at yourself in the mirror and realize you have already *become*. It's that moment when you understand that there is no one else needed to validate you because you walk in the security of knowing each and every single day that you wake and are able to say, "I am me, whole, healed, and free, choosing to love myself into destiny."

It doesn't matter who you are, how low you have been, or how high the platform you have been placed upon. You were bought with a price that no one could ever afford, except one: Jesus! Jesus died for this very moment right here, so you, the true you, authentic you, powerful you, breathtaking you, anointed, called, appointed, and chosen you could come forth and acknowledge the truth in all that God says about you and has shown you on this 30-day journey to seeing the unapologetic you!

Stop and Journal

#DAY29
#WHOLEHEALEDANDFREE

"And it is God who establishes us with you in Christ,
and has anointed us, and who has also put his seal on us
and given us his Spirit in our hearts as a guarantee."
(2 Corinthians 1:21-22 ESV)

JOURNAL #43: Write down what this is beginning to feel like
and look like to you.

Take a deep breath and realize who you are now...Right now!

Write down your meaning of each section below

I am Whole:

I am Healed:

I am Free:

It is well...

Someone once told me that you frame your world with the words that continue to come out of your mouth. If one of the hit BET shows hasn't taught me anything else, it has used the lead female character in a powerful way. She taught me to be comfortable in affirming myself, even if it's with Post-It notes on my mirror or door. I've also learned that we should no longer apologize for being gifted, powerful, strong, gorgeous, fearless, and unashamed of winning at what we do. There is no more: was, if, should've, could've, or would've. It's all been washed away.

When, you ask?

The moment you decided to pick up and read this book and take your journey.

How, you ask?

It was all a set-up, and a set-up from God himself since that very day he had me at my brother Harmony Samuels's studio, crying out to be free so I could finally love myself!

Why, you ask?

Simply because you're worth it! Take a deep breath and realize who you are now. *Right now!*

I am:

Whole

Adjective: 1. all of; entire, complete, full, unabridged, uncut
2. in an unbroken or undamaged state; in one piece

Noun: 1. a thing that is complete in itself
2. all of something [All!]

Healed

Verb: 1. to become sound or healthy again—recover, mend, improve
2. alleviate (a person's distress or anguish)

Free

Adjective: 1. Not under the control or in the power of another; able to act or be done as one wishes
2. not physically restrained, obstructed, or fixed; unimpeded: unimpeded, unobstructed, unrestricted, unhampered, clear, open, unblocked

Verb: 1. Release from captivity, confinement, or slavery. Release, set free, let go, liberate, discharge, deliver; set loose, let loose, turn loose, untie, unchain, unfetter, unshackle, unleash (www.Google.com Definitions)

It is well...

DAY 30

Neos "New Life" in Love

In this powerful moment, I heard the Holy Spirit speak to my spirit and say,

"Look up and realize that, all along, you were in love with yourself, but just didn't quite understand that. You expected people to understand and accept what you never took the time to do either, just for you. Now you know you are worth it, and through this, you were able to see the moments where you truly chose to love yourself over everything. You picked up this book in faith, knowing and believing that I would sustain you and that this was your time."

"You are right on time! It is your time, and with you trusting the process to becoming whole, healed, and free as you step into destiny, I have positioned all of heaven and my angels to cover you, protect you, keep you, and sustain you as you keep your eyes cast up, never looking back. We have you, and your story is beginning to unfold in the way you, along with everyone else, have never seen before. I believe in you. This is your destiny, given to you by me, for you were the only one I could choose to go forth with me on this undefined journey. It's your time, beloved."

"This is love. You have finally found it in me so I could define it unconditionally in you. Your whole life is about to change, and I need you to keep journaling, for this is developing your story that shall become a part of your legacy. Thank you for loving me and falling in love with everything concerning yourself that is approved, called, chosen, and destined by me, limitlessly."

On day 30, God has elated your presence in his glory, in a way that no one may ever be able to understand. But all that matters is that you've made it! He defined his *process* in you *resting* throughout

167

the *defining moments* of *the truth* and the understanding that *it is real*. Your *true breakthrough* was in *the process* of understanding your *power in patience*, in the midst of *the attack of your joy* through *the fight*, and your *fear unconfined*.

As you were *searching* and *realizing what had died*, you may have been *wounded but not broken*, knowing that *it isn't your fault*. And with *nothing left to give*, you received *the revelation*. In that, *the breakthrough* came. You began *believing again*, standing, and being *fearless* with your *unfailing faith*. You understood the reality in knowing *what it really means to be okay and better*, taking it *one day at a time* as you were *beginning to fall in love with God and learning how to fall in love with yourself*, along with *unconditionally loving others*.

There is freedom in *leaning not unto thine own understanding* and standing firm in knowing what "*I am more than enough*" really feels like, lives like, sounds like, walks like, speaks like, and shines like. What was so costly but so edifying was the point when you understood the essence of the question: *who am I, God, that you are mindful of me?* As you dashed into the *secret place*, some in contemplation, you understood the true definition of *I am me* in being *whole, healed, and free* as you wake up, creating a new history in your destiny with the fullness of *neos "new life" in love*.

This is your story! Now, it's time for you to write yours.

You are free to be *whole, healed, and free* to *step into destiny*. Now, when you look in the mirror, you can see all the beauty that has been birthed through every season and every day of this journey. It is no longer suppressed but drawn to the surface for the world to see what God means when his living Word says, "And God saw every thing that he made, and, behold, it was very good…" (Genesis 1:31, KJV)

Now, it's your time to begin to write your story!
Amen!

God's everlasting love:

> What then shall we say to these things? If God
> be for us, who can be against us? He who did not
> spare His own Son, but delivered Him up for us

all, how shall He not with Him also freely give us all things? Who shall bring a charge against God's elect? It is God who justifies. Who is he who condemns? It is Christ who died, and furthermore is also risen, who is even at the right hand of God, who also makes intercession for us. Who shall separate us from the love of Christ? Shall tribulation, or distress, or persecution, or famine, or nakedness, or peril, or sword? As it is written: "For your sake we are killed a; day long; We are accounted as sheep for slaughter." Yet in all these things we are more than conquerors through Him who loved us. For I am persuaded that neither death nor life, nor angels nor principalities, nor powers, nor things present nor things to come, nor height nor depth, nor any other created thing, shall be able to separate us form the love of God which is in Christ Jesus our Lord. (Romans 8:31–39, KJV)

It is finished!

Stop and Journal

#DAY30
#NEOSNEWLIFEINLOVE

"Look up and realize that all along you were in love with yourself, but you just didn't quite understand yourself. In that, you expected people to understand and accept what you never took the time to do either: just for you. Now, you know you are worth it, and through this, you were able to see the moments where you truly chose to love yourself over everything.

You picked up this book in faith, knowing and believing that I would sustain you and that this was your time. You are right on time! It is your time, and with you trusting the process to becoming whole, healed, and free as you step into destiny, I have positioned all of Heaven and my angels to cover you, protect you, keep you, and sustain you as you keep your eyes cast above; never, ever look back. We have you, and your story is beginning to unfold in the way you, along with anyone else, has ever seen before.

I believe in you, and this is your destiny, given to you by me because you were the only one I could choose to go forth—with me—on this undefined journey. It's your time, beloved. This is love, and you have finally found it in me so that I could define it unconditionally in you. Your whole life is about to change, and I need you to keep journaling, for this is developing your story that shall become a part of your legacy.

Thank you for loving me and falling in love with everything concerning yourself that is approved, called, chosen, and destined by Me, limitlessly."

Love, God

"And God saw every thing that he made,
and, behold, it was very good..."
(Genesis 1:31 KJV)

Now it's your time to begin to write your story!
Amen!

Additional Resources

I am so grateful for the dynamic pieces of truth that helped me along my journey to writing this empowering book of deliverance for women. These sources kept me, sustained me, and helped birth the perfect tool to reach women all over this nation and world.

Thank you for your work that I could embrace and use to support mine.

Read *Produced by Faith* by Devon Franklin
It breaks down the importance of *resting*

Go to:

("Bible Verses for When You Feel Not Good Enough"
by Rachel Wojnarowski July 18th, 2013. www.rachelwojo.com)
"What Are Defining Moments" www.reallifepurpose.org

ACKNOWLEDGMENTS

Wow! I first have to thank, with all of my heart, body, spirit and soul, my *Lord and Savior Jesus Christ* for loving me, molding me, shaping me, breaking me, building me, sustaining me, keeping me, cultivating me, encouraging me, and speaking into me day in and day out. He has never been silent to any of my tears. He has given me the greatest understanding of who I am, in him and has taught me how to accept, love and understand me unconditionally and unapologetically. If he didn't choose me, approve me, call me, and anoint me for such a destiny as the one I am living, I wouldn't know what it ever meant to be *free in being me.* Thank you, Jesus, for healing me, making me whole and setting me free to live out the greatest dream that I once before wasn't even able to believe. I love you, Jesus! You are my everything, and today more than ever I know what that means.

My beautiful parents! *Mommy, Donna J. Banks and Poppy, Pastor Robert C. Banks,* with tears I stand here today saying God couldn't have handpicked any greater parents for me than you two. I'm praying one day soon I can take care of you the way you have cultivated and taken care of me in and out of destiny, in and out of the doctor's office, in and out of heartbreaks in broken relationships, on and off the road, stages and sets, and in and out of my greatest triumphs and sacrifices. My God, your prayers without ceasing, to our Heavenly father have picked me up and held me close to his bosom. Thank you for raising me up in Jesus. Here I stand *Mommy and Poppy* in my true identity, birthing this journey that you helped me to see as you guided me into worship and helped me to identify his glory in all things. I love you. I love you! All you have sacrificed my God was for such a time as this. Thank you for never allowing me to give up and for believing in me when I didn't know how to believe in myself.

My sissies Shawnda C. Smith Banks and Victoria L. Banks, you two have held me in your arms in the natural, in the spirit and in Gods truth. Sissies, I believe in you, and I see you as God sees you. I absolutely love you with all my heart. Thank you, sissy Shawn Shawn, for my nephew Kailon "My Boots" McCoy, and niece Hailey Madison "My Peaches" McCoy. Thank you, sissy Vicky, for my nieces Holly Ryan "My Cupcake/Mini Me" Torres and Taylor Ivy "My Sunflower" Walker. Always remember my anointed little ones, "You can do all things through Christ Jesus who strengthens you." (Philippian's 4:13). If words could only express, how much I love you and how you keep me going each day I wake.

My grandparents: My grammy (Great Grandma), my grand-daddy, Volley Lockett and Grandmommy Mae Lockett, my grandma Aletha "Betty" Henderson, my grandpa Gary Banks and Nana Janet Banks; your support, and love has helped me to stay faithful to God and his calling for my life. You believed in me, and I love you so much. I hold onto your words from Jesus daily. Never taking a moment I spend with you for granted, with tears I say I love you.

My God-Mommy/Auntie Wanda Lockett, yes I am getting emotional right now. You are the living proof of staying faithful to the work of God's kingdom coming on earth as it is in heaven. Your prayers, our talks, your hugs and faith bless my soul. God-Mommy, thank you for seeing me for me and never expecting anything from me but just being Reyna Joy. God truly spoke to you when he gave you my name "Reyna" equals Queen equals Peaceful One; Joy equals everlasting joy in Jesus. You inspire me each and every day God-Mommy to be the best me I can be as you are continually.

My pastor/spiritual father/uncle and angel, Pastor Charles "Chuck" Singleton of Loveland Church, man oh man. Here we are as close as a button stitched to an unbreakable piece of fabric since I was three years old. God knew what he was doing when he guided my parents to place us all under the dynamic covering and your pow-erful preaching at Loveland church. God used you to set the tone for my foundation of faith because he knew where, what, and all he had called me to. No matter what time or day you have been there for "Your Snowa" as a listening ear, praying warrior, even drying my tears and always making sure I knew you were near. The Holy Spirit prophetically spoke to you on how to help me spread my wings so I could fly and never die. I could say so much, but I love you so much Uncle, and I thank God for my Auntie Pastor Charlyn Singleton for allowing our bond to be built up and never broken down. I love you so much Auntie. My Singleton brothers, Chucky, Chris, Corey, and Carey, with all my heart I humbly say I absolutely love you and thank you for helping raise me up to be the Reyna Joy I am today. I believe in each of you.

My spiritual mom, Marie "Turtledove" Brewington, you watched me from the sidelines listening to the mighty voice of God from ages three until you heard his voice. Then you took your rightful place when I was eighteen, holding me still 'till this very day. You have cried with me, wiped my tears, held me, checked me, prayed stronghold breaking prayers over me and helped me die so I could begin to finally live free. You taught me real love so I could finally understand my Heavenly father's love. He used you to assist him in healing many wounds that half the time I didn't know were even there. Turtledove, I love you and forever., I will praise God for you my angel.

Loveland Church, each of you have watched me from the beginning of time and supported me in and out of every season. Your love runs deep, and I thank you for all of your prayers and endless love.

My auntie's, uncle's, and cousin's, all of you, I love you deeply. Never to take your presence in my life and destiny for granted. Aunt Sandy and Uncle Al Williams, your love and faith in me has helped me stand against the fire. I love you deeply. My Baby Cuzzy's, Lacy "Lay Lay Banks, Olicia "LiLi" Williams, Autumn "Autchum Botchum" Morris, I believe in you, and you are destined for the greatest calling in history. Stay in it my baby cousin's, stay in it. I'm here for you.

My spiritual daughter Keya Vance and Quantinique Hurd, I love you with every bit of love God has placed within me to give to you both. My baby girls and baby angels, I am so proud of you. Thank you for your unconditional love.

My mentor Faune Chambers Watkins, all I can say for all of Heaven and the world to see is Faune, God used you directly in three main seasons to save my entire life and destiny. I was afraid of the mantle I was called to carry, and in that he gave you permission to help keep me from running away from the call as you began walking with me through my pain to help carry me until the weight of it became second nature to me. I stopped living in pain to live in Gods healing. Our tears were not in van sissy. Look at God, beloved.

My sissy Meagan Good Franklin, and my brother Devon Franklin, I love you two angelic presence in my life. Sissy, you have embraced me since the day we met, and you looked at me and said, "You are wow beautiful, and I see your heart., It's breathtaking., I see you, Reyna." Since that day, you have stood with me and sowed into my destiny with your love, hugs, emoji's, talks, and heart. Brother your preaching and words of encouragement have given me the fire from God to do destiny. God used you to keep me from apologizing for being called by God. Here, I stand fear- free and so alive in Jesus our Lord! Love you two so much. Thank you for covering and cultivating me.

My previous life coach, Karen Norwood, I praise God for speaking to Harmony Samuels that special day as he sent me to you. I am humbled and grateful for you taking me in each week and being a huge part of the birthing of this book and my journey to being healed in wholeness with full forgiveness of Reyna Joy Banks. In God using you, you gave me permission in Christ to release every iniquity and shed every broken piece of who I thought I was supposed to be. I love you for taking time to kill off the enemy's plans to keep me from becoming me.

My auntie Deborah Smith Pegues as a multiple New York Times Bestseller and full- time destiny builder, you took the time to sit with me, feed me spiritually, mentally, physically, and emotionally as I prepared to turn my journey into this life-changing book for women. Your love is contagious, and so many have been affected through your love for Christ and people all over this world. I love you so very much.

My DeEtta "Mama Dee" West, you are my angel and special covering since I was elven and while I was in Atlanta, Georgia. What a woman of wisdom, power, honor, and love under God's anointing. I love you angel, and I pray major favor and blessings upon you beyond what you have room to receive.

My dance babies, all over this nation and world, you know exactly who you are I am screaming I love you, and I am here for you forever and always; the journey has just begun beloveds.

My besties: Krista Ornelas, Caryn Brown, Deorlean Claiborne, Michele Weaver, Brittany Jackson, Meiko Taylor and Cousin/Twin Mylin Elizabeth, with tears I simply, with a whole heart say thank you, and I love you so much. We are whole, healed and free living life more abundantly. My God, never have we seen the righteous forsaken.

All of my sissies in Christ, Sister Keepers, destiny builders and stronghold breakers, you each know exactly who you are. Thank you for fighting for me, with me.

My agents (Lisa Lindholm, Terry Lindholm and the entire Go2Talent Agency Family, former agency Trio Talent Agency), I praise God for you daily. Lisa, you believed in me and always made time for me in the midst of my transitions and heart for God's Kingdom.

AZ FILMZ (Partnered Production Company), Zeus Zeus and Al Al; Thank you for your yes to every vision we have brought your way. For seeing me through Gods eyes and holding my hand on this journey to truly changing the world as God has called us to do so with our gifts in every way. Working with you has changed my life ad so many others lives. I began to dream again and believe in myself again because you helped me to see my power within. Thank you for being our angels and there is so much more history to be made and magic to create for his glory! I love you both so very much, lets keep hanging the game through releasing the sound of Gods love like never before. Cheers to everything new, great, bold and world changing.

Tiana Kocher (Recording Artist/Songwriter/Actress), Katrina Ponce Enrile and Manila Music Label, your trust, love and faith has blessed my entire life these past few years in ways I can't even describe. Your ability to endure and overcome through all that comes your way in the midst of pressing into your dreams is breathtaking! Baby T we believe in you and your time is now. Thank you for allowing myself, FHG Entertainment and 2 LIVVV to pour into what God has called you to in order to affect the generations through your music and change the entire world through your greatest gift to LOVE past your own understanding. We salute you and I am forever excited to share this journey called life with you angels. Mom your sowing and sacrifice is not on vain get ready to reap your harvest angel.

BOE Global, thank you for all the love and support you showed me in my calling and gifting. Major. Is going all the way to the top, and I pray everything you guys touch turns to gold. I love each of you. Thank you Harmony Samuels for birthing something so world changing, "Best Of Everything" literally.

Special thank you to my heart, Dr. Holly Carter at Relevé Entertainment. You and Mr. PK's faith in God's calling upon my life as you trust me to bring your visions to life. The Merge Summit and Ascend Bible Study with you, Ms. Robi Reed and my Tracy Blackwell has been used by God to take me to a new level in destiny, like never before. So humbled to have each of you in my life and so honored. I love you. My brother in my career and calling Cee Barrett, you walked with me through the darkest season. I love you brother, and I am so proud of you. God favors you in so many ways.

All the Partners, Legacy Builders and Artist's of F.H.G. "For His Glory" Entertainment Family (you each know who you are since the birthing of this call), I love you, and it is time for us to bring down his glory. God needs us to stay standing, become unshakable and unwavering. It's time to stir up a revival For His Glory. Partner's: Dance 2 Livvv Tour, Team Spider Web (Joel Daley Web Designing Company and team), Kingdom Tak Ova (Jamecia), "Fearless Attire and Fearless Daughters"s (Brittany Salsberry), "Dreams Alive Club" (Tepsi and Family in Gaborone, Botswana Africa), "RED 12 Tulsa," IDA Hollywood "Gospel Youth Musec Organization" (Arreasha and Willette in Columbus, Ga.) Let's go and never stop the momentum. Watch God move but don't miss him when he does. Stay in it, we are one. I love each of you so much, my God I do.

This is beyond one of the most honored and humbled "Thank You" I can give, is to Christian Faith Publishing for seeing this manuscript and blueprint to women becoming whole, healed, and free as they begin to step into destiny.

Thank you, and I love my angels on earth!

ABOUT THE AUTHOR

Reyna is currently a creative director, choreographer, artist developer, artist manager, and CEO of four businesses. While being born and raised in the church, Reyna understands the need for her presence and gift to be experienced beyond church services and ministry as we've commonly known it. With over nineteen years of experience as a celebrity dancer, she noticed her life's purpose was beyond the world of dance. Public speaking and preaching was a natural addition to her life. From conferences to dance tours, Grammy stages, or music videos, Reyna has no limits.

She has shared stages and has worked with legends such as Beyonce, Ne-Yo, Justin Bieber, Toni Braxton, Chaka Khan, Dietrick Haddon, Usher Raymond, Kierra Sheard, MAJOR, Trinitee Stokes, Tiana Kocher, Michelle Williams, and even Travis Green, to name a few. She doesn't take lightly to the fact that she is trusted to work with artist who are changing the face of the music industry while she takes her place as a gatekeeper for what is happening next in art and entertainment.

Seeking not to make a name for herself, it's "for his glory." As a kingdom strategist she moves and leads with grace and poise. Her presence and her ability to cover, cultivate, connect, create, and catapult artists is what sets her in high places amongst the great. Her journey helped birth her non-profit, 2LIVVV. Through this endeavor, she can provide artists with a private, developmental experience that will enable them to shine publicly while no longer struggling to live out their designed legacy.

She is a devoted kingdom builder, author, speaker, creative director, choreographer, voiceover actress, host in radio/TV, and successful business professional. Surrounded by a family and community of faith and love in Los Angeles, California to the nations worldwide, Reyna seeks to help artists and every person she comes in contact with not to merely exist from day-to-day, but 2 LIVVV on purpose.

CPSIA information can be obtained
at www.ICGtesting.com
Printed in the USA
FSHW010728071119
63761FS

9 781644 922125